ARMS CONTROL AGREEMENTS

ARMS CONTROL AGREEMENTS

DESIGNS FOR VERIFICATION AND ORGANIZATION

DAVID W. WAINHOUSE

in association with

BERNHARD G. BECHHOEFER,

HARRY D. HUGHES, BYRON V. LEARY,

THEODORE ROCKWELL III, ANNE P. SIMONS,

and ARNOLD WOLFERS

The Johns Hopkins Press, Baltimore, Maryland

FOREWORD

Since World War II there have been more or less continuous international discussions and negotiations on arms control agreements. The study and planning of such agreements have become a regular, institutionalized part of the U.S. government's foreign policy activities. Although few arms agreements have been achieved, they will continue to command the attention of governments as long as the costs and dangers of arms competition cause concern.

One of the obstacles to achieving arms agreements—and it is an obstacle greatly enhanced by the technology of the nuclear age—arises from the difficulty of verifying the compliance or noncompliance of signatories. Any serious arms control program must pay scrupulous, detailed attention to the enormous technical and political problems that verification involves. This study examines with unique thoroughness some of the practical problems of organizing verification. In the process it also shows much about the real scope and limits of arms control.

This book is a revision and condensation of a study initially prepared by the Washington Center of Foreign Policy Research under a contract for the United States Arms Control and Disarmament Agency. The preparation and editing of the manuscript for publication was undertaken by William E. Butler, to whom the author and his associates are greatly indebted.

The views and judgments set forth in this book are solely those of the author and his associates and do not necessarily reflect the views of the United States Arms Control and Disarmament Agency or any other department or agency of the United States government.

June, 1968

ROBERT E. OSGOOD
Director
Washington Center of Foreign
Policy Research

CONTENTS

ABBREVIATIONS

ACDA   U.S. Arms Control and Disarmament Agency
AEC   U.S. Atomic Energy Commission
CENTO   Central Treaty Organization
ENDC   Eighteen Nation Disarmament Committee
FRG   Federal Republic of Germany
GC   General Conference of the IAEA
GCD   general and complete disarmament
GDR   German Democratic Republic
IAEA   International Atomic Energy Agency
IDO   International Disarmament Organization
LASA   Large Aperture Seismic Array
LIDO   Limited International Disarmament Organization
NATO   North Atlantic Treaty Organization
NFS   Nuclear Fuel Services, Inc.
OAS   Organization of American States
OAU   Organization of African Unity
PV   Procés Verbale

BIOGRAPHICAL NOTES

DAVID W. WAINHOUSE, Research Associate of the Washington Center for Foreign Policy Research, was formerly Deputy Assistant Secretary of State for U.N. Affairs and U.S. Minister to Austria. His publications include a *History of American Foreign Policy, Remnants of Empire* and *International Peace Observation.*

BERNHARD G. BECHHOEFER, former State Department official, adviser to U.S. disarmament delegations, and Research Associate of the Center on special assignment, is the author of *Postwar Negotiations for Arms Control,* numerous articles on the international control of atomic energy, and a contributor to *International Peace Observation.*

HARRY D. HUGHES is currently engaged in the private practice of law in Maryland. His experience includes many years service with governmental agencies.

GEN. BYRON V. LEARY (USMC, Ret.) was Deputy (later Acting) Chief of Staff of the United Nations Truce Supervision Organization in Palestine. He has been a Consultant and Research Associate of the Center on special assignment.

THEODORE ROCKWELL III is Director of MPR Associates, a Washington engineering firm. He previously served with the Manhattan Project, Oak Ridge, Tenn. and as Technical Director, Naval Reactors Headquarters. His publications include *The Reactor Shielding Design Manual, The Shippingport Pressurized Reactor,* and others in the field of nuclear power.

ANNE P. SIMONS, former member of the U.N. Secretariat, is co-author of *The United Nations and the Maintenance of International Peace and Security* and *The United States and the United Nations: The Search for International Peace and Security;* and Research Associate of the Center on special assignment.

ARNOLD WOLFERS is Sterling Professor Emeritus of International Relations, Yale University and former Director of the Washington Center of Foreign Policy Research. His publications include: *Britain and France between the Two Wars, Developments in Military Technology and Their Impact on U.S. Strategy and Foreign Policy,* and *Discord and Collaboration.*

ARMS CONTROL AGREEMENTS

INTRODUCTION

Since the failure to get the Baruch comprehensive atomic energy control plan accepted in the mid 1940's and early 1950's, the great powers have turned to partial measures of arms control or disarmament in the Eighteen Nation Disarmament Committee (ENDC). Several proposals for such measures are analyzed in this volume. The United States has also stated that it is prepared to discuss proposals for the exchange of military missions and for a system of observation posts to reduce the danger of war by accident, miscalculation, or surprise. The 1963 Limited Nuclear Test Ban Treaty prohibits nuclear testing in outer space, the atmosphere, and underwater. An outer space treaty which entered into force in October 1967 prohibits the orbiting and stationing of nuclear weapons in outer space and on celestial bodies. A treaty for a Latin American Nuclear Free Zone promises to prevent a nuclear arms race in a prescribed zone.

This piecemeal approach to halting the arms race suggests that there are specific areas in the armaments field which might be limited on a mutually acceptable basis. Each requires differing degrees of verification and access to ensure compliance. Once the processes of arms control are set in motion, mutual confidence might grow and the original arrangements give way to more comprehensive ones. This is not to overlook the issues which transcend East-West differences with respect to verification, but the very question of verification has tended to prevent agreement on arms control measures, especially when on-site inspection is involved.

No inspection system can be perfect or foolproof. Perfection is not attainable given the frailties of man and the complexities of technology. Technical systems can malfunction; human beings err. On the other hand, certain inspection schemes are more effective than others. The overriding criterion must be a verification system that adequately protects the interests of the parties to the agreement.

Within this criterion, the system should provide a framework sufficiently flexible to be modified as technical requirements change. To encourage the building of confidence, it is important not to set an unattainable goal. No one can hope to foresee in detail all the problems that might arise. Yet, if agreement on objectives can be attained, even a relatively modest verification system might develop a reasonably effective *modus operandi.*

Finally, one must prepare for the transition from a bipolar approach to arms control to one based on a diffusion of power centers. Partial measures agreements must be kept under continuous evaluation as the balance of forces changes. For example, the inclusion of mainland China and France would be an important condition to the long-term success of such agreements.

The purpose of this volume is to analyze, evaluate, and project international systems for verifying compliance with arms control and disarmament agreements.

Part I examines four important cases, three of which relate to nuclear arms, and the fourth to a first stage of general and complete disarmament (GCD). These four cases are examined because they concentrate on the crucial issues involved in arms control agreements. The cases are (1) the U.S. proposal for a verified agreement to halt production of fissionable materials for weapons purposes; (2) the Gomulka Proposals and the Rapacki Plan; (3) the U.S. proposal for a verified freeze of the number and characteristics of strategic nuclear offensive and defensive vehicles; and (4) the verification of Stage I of the proposals for GCD.

1. The first of these cases examined in this volume—a verified agreement to halt all production of fissionable materials for weapons use—deals with a proposal submitted to the ENDC by the United States on January 21, 1964. It is a proposal of a far-reaching character in that it

seeks to limit the amount of explosive materials available for nuclear weapons and would at the same time permit the production of fissionable materials for peaceful purposes. Verification would be lodged largely with the International Atomic Energy Agency (IAEA).

A major purpose of this partial measure of arms control is to halt the proliferation of nuclear weapons and weapon technology to those nations not now having nuclear weapons in order to reduce the threat to peace and security. It is the view of the United States, which the United Kingdom and the Soviet Union share, that "every increase in the number of nations controlling nuclear weapons will multiply the possibilities of nuclear confrontations and the risks of accidental or intentional use of nuclear weapons."[1] The spread of nuclear weapons to other states cannot but decrease the security of the non-nuclear states and the "acquisition of nuclear weapons by smaller countries would increase the likelihood of the great powers' becoming involved in what otherwise might remain local conflicts."[2]

The proposal to halt the production of fissionable material is in some respects similar to, and in others different from, one aspect of the agreed draft of a non-proliferation treaty tabled by the United States and the Soviet Union at the ENDC in March 1968.

The draft of the non-proliferation treaty obliges non-nuclear states to accept the proposed safeguards, but not the nuclear powers. On December 2, 1967, President Johnson, on the occasion of the 25th anniversary of the first atomic chain reaction, announced that the United States, when and if the non-proliferation treaty goes into effect, "will permit the IAEA to apply its safeguards to all nuclear activities in the United States—excluding only those with direct national security significance."[3] Under this offer, the IAEA will be able to inspect "a broad range of U.S. nuclear activities, both governmental and private, including the fuel in nuclear-power reactors owned by utilities for generating electricity, and the fabrication and chemical reprocessing of such fuels,"[4] the President asserted. He made it clear that the United States is not asking any country to accept safeguards that it is unwilling to accept itself, and invited the nations of the world to join in. It is doubtful whether the Soviet Union will respond to this appeal in the light of its long-standing aversion to on-site inspection.

One serious problem related to the non-proliferation treaty has been raised by some non-nuclear states, all of whom are being asked to forego acquiring nuclear weapons. What if a non-nuclear country becomes the object of a threat of nuclear attack or blackmail? Would the nuclear powers be prepared to guarantee not to use or threaten to use such weapons against non-nuclear states in all circumstances? In addition to this self-denying ordinance, what would the nuclear powers do if

3

one of them violated its commitment? These are some of the questions which non-nuclear states are asking.

The President has on several occasions spoken out on the question of a threat of nuclear blackmail. On October 18, 1964, for example, on the occasion of the first Chinese nuclear explosion, President Johnson stated: "The nations that do not seek national nuclear weapons can be sure that, if they need our strong support against some threat of nuclear blackmail, then they will have it."[5] A Presidential policy statement of this character is unilateral and not in the nature of a treaty obligation. As one writer put it: "The force of a unilateral policy expressed in sufficient detail to make clear that it will be a basis for future action should not be underestimated, nor should the binding character of a guarantee in treaty form be overestimated."[6]

It appears clear from the discussions in the ENDC and in the United Nations that the non-proliferation treaty tabled by the United States and the Soviet Union or a separate treaty will need to embody the concept of an acceptable balance of the mutual responsibilities and obligations of the nuclear and non-nuclear states.[7]

If these problems can be resolved, it will be necessary to develop and expand expeditiously the IAEA verification organization to cope with the rapid spread of nuclear facilities producing ever increasing quantities of fissionable material which can be converted to nuclear weapons.

How this could be done in the more difficult case—that of the proposal for a halt in the production of fissionable materials for weapons uses—is examined in the first case study in this volume.

2. The second case examined includes the Gomulka Proposals and the Rapacki Plan. There have been several variants of the latter; the one considered here was submitted by Poland's Foreign Minister, Adam Rapacki, in the ENDC on March 28, 1962.[8] It provides for the elimination of nuclear weapons and the means of delivering them and the reduction of armed forces and conventional armaments within the limited area of the Federal Republic of Germany (FRG), the German Democratic Republic (GDR), Czechoslovakia, and Poland. The nuclear ban would also be binding on the four nuclear powers, the Soviet Union, the United States, the United Kingdom, and France which maintain forces in the territories of these countries. The proposal calls for a verification system to ensure compliance.

A less complicated variant of the Rapacki Plan is the Gomulka Proposals,[9] submitted to the governments concerned on February 29, 1964. It proposes a freeze of the existing nuclear *status quo* in the same geographical area and a control system to verify compliance composed of the representatives of the Warsaw Pact and NATO countries on a parity basis. Unlike the Rapacki proposal, the Gomulka Proposals do not deal with conventional arms nor with armed forces.

The nuclear-free zone concept has been the subject of discussion in the United Nations and elsewhere since 1956 and has related to areas such as the Middle East, the Balkans, Africa, and Latin America. Only in the Latin American area has the concept found concrete expression. In Mexico City fourteen Latin American governments on February 14, 1967 signed the Treaty for the Prohibition of Nuclear Weapons in Latin America. This is the first nuclear free-zone treaty for an inhabited area of the world and constitutes a landmark in man's quest to limit the nuclear arms race. It is of interest to note what the United Nations Secretary-General said on the occasion of the successful conclusion of its negotiation:

The provisions of the Treaty also mark a major step forward in the field of verification and control. Among the treaties I have mentioned [the Antarctic Treaty of 1959, the Nuclear Test Ban Treaty of 1963, and the Outer Space Treaty of January 1967] the one you have to-day approved is the first and only one that establishes an effective system of control, under a permanent and supervisory organ. By adopting the safeguards system of the International Atomic Energy Agency and by setting up a system of special inspections in case of suspicion, outside of the Agency's safeguards system, of violation, you have also pioneered the way in providing a sound method of assurance to all parties that the Treaty will be observed.[10]

While the United States and its allies have approached the nuclear-free zone concept chiefly in terms of preventing multiplication of nuclear powers, the Soviet Union and its allies have generally called for keeping areas in various parts of the world, particularly in Central Europe, completely free from nuclear weapons. The expression of that aim is to be found in the Rapacki Plan and the Gomulka Proposals.

A nuclear-free zone in Central Europe raises a number of complex political problems which differ from those encountered in the Latin American treaty. Nuclear weapons are already present in the former, and some states have a far greater potential for converting fissionable materials into effective weapon systems than any Latin American states. Moreover, Central Europe is of greater strategic importance. An agreement for a nuclear-free zone in Central Europe would serve to prevent nuclear weapon proliferation. It would be an essential part of a broader East-West political and military détente.

3. The third case examined is the United States proposal for a freeze of strategic nuclear delivery vehicles which President Johnson urged upon the ENDC in January 1964.

The purpose in submitting this proposal, in the President's words, was "to halt further increases in strategic armaments now." He told the ENDC that "the security of all nations can be safeguarded within the scope of such an agreement, and that this initial measure, preventing the further expansion of the deadly and costly arms race, will open the path to reduction in all types of forces from present levels."[11]

In the view of the United States, this partial measure of arms control was singled out for consideration by the ENDC because the strategic nuclear vehicle is a weapon of the greatest destructiveness, the most costly to produce, and—in the words of the U.S. Representative to ENDC, William Foster—"a freeze on these weapons can be achieved with effective inspection requirements which would be less than those required for a general and complete disarmament program limiting all major armaments across the board."[12]

The analysis in this case study is directed both to the extent of verification which can be achieved and the organizational requirements for such verification.

4. The fourth case study is based upon proposals for GCD introduced by the Soviet Union and the United States in the spring of 1962. Such proposals are not new. The League of Nations and the United Nations have wrestled with the problem unsuccessfully for years.

Early discussions in the United Nations focused on international control of atomic energy and general disarmament. They resulted in repeated deadlocks between the Soviet Union and the Western Powers primarily over the issue of verification. After 1955, emphasis shifted to a search for partial measures of arms control that might dampen down the arms race.

Interest in GCD was revived in 1961 when the United States and the Soviet Union submitted to the United Nations General Assembly a "Joint Statement of Agreed Principles for Disarmament Negotiations." The statement was unanimously endorsed by the Assembly and an agreement was reached on a new negotiating forum—the ENDC.[13]

On March 15, 1962 the Soviet Union submitted to the ENDC a "Draft Treaty on General and Complete Disarmament Under Strict International Control." A month later the United States submitted its "Outline of Basic Provisions of a Treaty on General and Complete Disarmament in a Peaceful World." These two plans for accomplishing GCD through a process of three stages are the most comprehensive either government has ever introduced. The discussions on them in the ENDC are among the most extensive and concrete ever held on the subject of general disarmament.

At the outset, the ENDC decided that "concurrently with the elaboration of agreement on general and complete disarmament" it would consider "various proposals on the implementation of measures aimed at lessening international tension, consolidating confidence among States, and facilitating general and complete disarmament."[14] In more recent years, discussion on arms control has centered almost entirely on proposals for limited agreements of the latter type rather than on GCD.

Most of the proposals for partial measures, however, are identical with, or very similar, to the measures in the United States and Soviet plans for Stage I of GCD including the proposals analyzed in the first three case studies. The acceptance of several of these measures might require a verification system very similar to that which would be needed for Stage I.

Both the United States and Soviet plans call for the establishment of an International Disarmament Organization (IDO) to verify compliance with a general disarmament treaty. The comparative analysis contained in the fourth case study of the provisions concerning the structure, powers, and functions suggested for this organization is of considerable interest, not only because of the contrast between the approaches of the two superpowers toward a verification system but also what is disclosed concerning their attitudes toward international organizations in general.

Among the questions analyzed in these cases are the appropriate jurisdiction and functions of verification organizations; the allocation of verification functions between inspection systems under the control of the adversary and/or international systems; the problem of whether organizations should have functions beyond information gathering and dissemination, such as determining the existence of a violation or deciding or recommending responses to alleged or established violation of arms control and disarmament measures; the appropriate membership, structure and voting, or other decision-making procedures of such organizations; the number and types of organs; and the distribution of authority among such bodies.

Attention is also devoted to such problems as recruiting and retaining competent, impartial international personnel, the need for special qualifications or technical training, as well as for balanced representation of geographical areas and political systems on such a staff. Consideration is given to the relationship of a verification organization to other international organizations, including the United Nations, the International Atomic Energy Agency, and regional organizations.

In light of the problems considered in these case studies, and in light of the first-hand experience of some of the authors with international organizations and scientific and technical aspects of verification, Part II develops general principles pertaining to solutions of anticipated international organizational problems in the course of verifying compliance.

Also examined are such questions as the extent to which verification organs might be merged with, or become subsidiary to, organs of the United Nations or other existing international organizations and the degree to which autonomy for verification organizations is desirable.

In addition to general principles, Part II includes a proposal for, and analysis of, the feasibility and desirability of creating a single international verification organization that at a later date could assume some or all of the functions carried out by other organizations in these fields.

ORGANIZATIONAL ARRANGEMENTS
FOR VERIFYING ARMS CONTROL

THE U.S. PROPOSAL TO HALT PRODUCTION
OF FISSIONABLE MATERIALS
FOR WEAPONS PURPOSES

Verification of a "cutoff" agreement to halt production of fissionable materials for weapons use is based on the principle of accountability; that is, determining the amount of fissionable materials produced and tracing the purposes for which the materials are utilized. In this respect the cutoff is a lineal descendant of the first U.S. proposal, the so-called Baruch Plan, to eliminate nuclear weapons and to ensure the utilization of fissionable material solely for non-weapons purposes.

When the United States proposed the Baruch Plan in 1946 and was the only state producing fissionable materials, it was possible to account for all past and future production and therefore to ensure that such materials were not used for weapons. By 1953, production by the United States, the Soviet Union, and the United Kingdom had increased to such an extent that it was no longer possible to account for past production with sufficient accuracy to guarantee the elimination of nuclear weapons, although this was not officially recognized by the Soviet

Union and the United States until 1955.[1] Thereafter, discussions of arms limitations entailing verification were confined to future production. Although this could not eliminate the danger of nuclear war among powers with nuclear weapons, limitations on future production could assure that their stockpiles would not increase and that other states would not become nuclear powers.[2]

The safeguards system for a cutoff has not been elaborated upon in arms control negotiations. In 1962 the United Kingdom estimated in the ENDC the requirements for ensuring that production of fissionable materials would be utilized solely for peaceful purposes on a world-wide basis, and the United States, in June 1964, outlined such a safeguards system to the Committee. The American proposal (ENDC/134, June 26, 1964) is the point of departure in this study for an examination of international organizational arrangements to verify a cutoff.

Several assumptions should be made clear at the outset. First, the organization to police the cutoff would be built on the structure of the IAEA. Second, this study assumes a gradual improvement of Soviet-American relations over the course of the next ten years. No assumptions are made with regard to relations of either the United States or the Soviet Union toward other states such as France, Germany, or Communist China.

Any series of treaties embodying a cutoff would ultimately include a package of basic undertakings: (a) agreements among the United States, the United Kingdom, and the Soviet Union not to disseminate weapons information and not to transfer nuclear weapons to other states; (b) provisions for international transfer of fissionable materials under safeguards to assure their peaceful use; (c) provisions for the cutoff itself—no further production of fissionable materials for atomic weapons; and (d) international inspection of shut down facilities—reactors primarily for production of plutonium—as well as other facilities involved in production.

It is also assumed that certain technical considerations such as differences in the quality of the plutonium produced from various types of reactors would not alter the verification requirements, since all plutonium from power reactors has a weapons potential. The present increased value of plutonium for certain non-weapons uses produced by long irradiation also would not alter verification requirements, since a potential violator is not likely to be deterred by a premium price.[3]

Only modest progress has been achieved in the negotiation of a cutoff partly because the Soviet Union has assumed that the cutoff would entail a verification system involving intrusion disproportionate to its advantages. Estimates of some Western observers for an inspection force have ranged from 10,000 to 45,000. However, a careful analysis of the re-

PLUTONIUM PRODUCED BY CIVILIAN ATOMIC POWER STATIONS

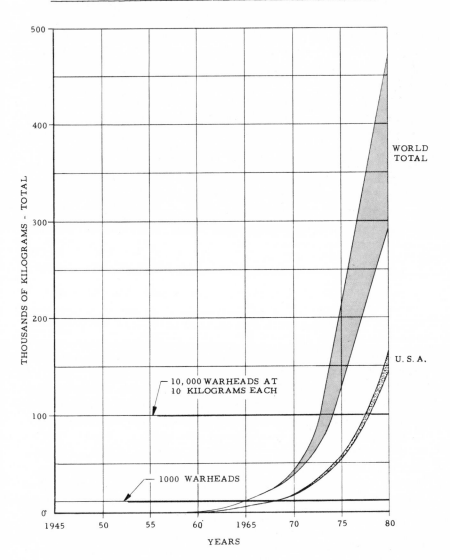

quirements for verification machinery suggests that verification can be attained in an organization substantially smaller than any heretofore suggested. Moreover, until recently it was believed that the production of fissionable material for non-weapons programs would be small in comparison with existing weapons stockpiles not affected by a cutoff and would not justify elaborate verification machinery. Recent technological developments, however, have enabled nuclear fuels to compete economically with conventional ones in certain areas of the world in the production of electric power. By 1980 it is projected that non-weapons uses will produce significant quantities of fissionable material even in relation to past stockpiles. The development of a weapons capability by France and Communist China underlines the importance of controlling proliferation of nuclear weapons before stockpiles are so widely dispersed that no accountability system can appreciably increase international safety.

This paper was prepared in light of these developments with a view to working out a verification scheme that would provide reasonable assurance of detecting violations and result in minimal intrusion into states with nuclear facilities.

Inspection under the IAEA

There is at present an inspection organization in the IAEA which is responsible for verifying the operation of a number of research and materials testing reactors, a few power reactors, and one commercial chemical fuel processing plant. The first question that arises is whether this system could be extended to cover all declared reactors anywhere in the world.

The task of inspecting reactors is simpler than dealing with other stages of the nuclear fuel cycle. The fuel element of a reactor generally contains either natural uranium or uranium with a low degree of enrichment. Since the fuel elements are sealed and are radioactively "hot," it would be difficult to remove either the uranium or plutonium content from the fuel elements at the reactor site. The fuel elements must cool off in a pool for months before it is safe to handle them. To separate the plutonium product requires complex processing not generally done at the reactor site. Thus, the possibility of diversion of either uranium or plutonium is slight. It would be possible to introduce into the reactors other materials which could be radioactivated and then withdrawn. However, operations data would go a long way toward detecting such efforts, and the quantity of additional materials which could be produced in this manner would be relatively small. It would indeed be a major effort to develop a bomb from this sort of diversion.

An increase in the number of reactors subject to inspection would not require a proportionate increase in the number of inspectors or supporting personnel. It is reasonable to conclude that the IAEA could be the instrumentality for verifying reactor operations anywhere in the world if a cutoff agreement should give the Agency this authority. In view of the large number of states possessing reactors as well as the necessity of utilizing the data as part of an international accountability system, reciprocal inspection of reactors would seem unsatisfactory.

Verification of Chemical Processing Plants

A chemical processing plant is one of the two stages of the nuclear fuel cycle where nuclear materials could most readily be diverted from peaceful to military uses. Upon the dissolution of the fuel elements and the separation of the contents into plutonium or U–233, uranium with varying enrichments of U–235, and waste products, the plutonium and U–233, and in some instances U–235, are in a form where they could be utilized for weapons. In the past, it was generally believed that exact verification of the production of a chemical separation plant presented vast difficulties. While it would be possible to measure the product of the plant accurately, an exact balance of the output with the fissionable material content of the input was the problem. Spent fuel rods are highly radioactive when they enter the plant, and it is impossible to make an accurate input measurement of the nuclear materials they contain. In lieu of accurate input measurements, an estimate is made based upon the design of the reactor where the fuel elements were utilized and its performance record. It is thus possible to predict the uranium and plutonium content of the fuel rods. Recent developments, however, have considerably simplified the problem of attaining accurate accountability in a chemical processing plant.

In 1966 the U.S. AEC reached an agreement with the IAEA permitting it to inspect the first commercial chemical processing plant in the world—the plant of Nuclear Fuel Services, Inc., (NFS) at West Valley, N.Y. The decision to utilize an international organization to inspect the first commercial chemical processing plant reflects the fact that the technology is in the public domain. The Commission authorized NFS to prepare as a research project a *Safeguard Procedures Manual for the NFS Reprocessing Plant*. After completion of the Manual in February 1967, discussions with IAEA resulted in agreement on the safeguards procedures. The first fuels subject to IAEA safeguards were actually processed and the safeguards successfully applied in August 1967.

Previous studies on safeguarding chemical processing operations have become largely outdated by the results of the NFS study. This study was prepared under the direction of Dr. R. P. Wischow, at that time

Director of Research and Development at NFS, and summarized by Dr. Wischow and Dr. W. A. Rodger on June 26, 1967, at the Symposium on Safeguards and Development at the Argonne National Laboratories in Illinois.[4]

The safeguards system developed for NFS confirms the validity of the U.S. approach to this problem in the ENDC. The three main features of the United States position were review of design, maintenance of adequate records and reports, and inspection of physical surroundings.

The NFS plant design lends itself readily to the application of safeguards procedures. The NFS plant ordinarily will not operate for more than twenty-five or thirty days without shutting down to account for materials which may have stuck to the pipes or other portions of the plant. Under this method of operation, discrepancies between the input and the output will be detected quickly, and investigations can be made to determine the cause. This is not possible in the Hanford and Savannah River plants where operations are almost continuous, and the plants are not cleaned out more than once a year. Furthermore, the NFS plant permits visual observation of most of its operations and the obtaining of samples at all stages. The IAEA procedures fully utilize these favorable features and call for many samples, as well as Polaroid photographs of significant operations. These design features arose primarily as a result of commercial considerations: the necessity of separating the varying nuclear materials of several customers. However, they do also facilitate inspection.

The IAEA inspection system relies primarily on the second and third features suggested in the ENDC paper submitted by the United States: accountability and surveillance. The NFS accountability program is capable of accounting within plus or minus 2 percent of the plant throughput. The suggested procedures are intended to determine with an assumed 95 percent confidence level that a nondetected diversion of nuclear materials would be less than the uncertainties of the accountability program. This leaves something to be desired, since 2 percent of the throughput would still be a sizable amount of fissionable material. However, the Argonne paper shows that a bias would become apparent if the entire amount were diverted. The safeguards program would thus be capable of detecting, if not preventing, diversion. The accountability and physical security measures, however, might discourage a would-be diverter by convincing him his actions would be detected.

The Argonne paper recommended a resident staff of eighteen, at a cost of $500,000 annually, to safeguard the entire production of the NFS plant. This is in contrast to the staff of ten assigned by IAEA for the initial inspection. This recommendation, however, "was directed towards an inspection of an isolated fuels reprocessing plant and not a plant that was part of an overall safeguarded fuel cycle complex," a situation that would exist in the event of a cutoff. The Argonne paper concluded that "many more people are required to safeguard an independent facility than would be required for the same facility that was part of a fully safeguarded nuclear fuel cycle. In the latter case, a true system of audit or checks and balances could be effectively utilized to verify whether or not a diversion has occurred."[5]

The estimated personnel and costs for inspection of the NFS plant are substantially less than the manpower and cost estimates suggested by earlier studies. For example, a study by the Vitro Corporation suggested twenty-nine inspectors, a capital cost (in 1956 dollars) of $724,500, and an annual operating cost of $1,034,000 for a smaller complex of power reactors and chemical processing plants. This would be between 15 and 20 percent of the total anticipated annual operating costs of the complex described in the Vitro report as compared to a safeguards cost not to exceed 5 percent of operating costs of NFS. The primary reason for the high costs and personnel requirements is that the Vitro report contemplated that the IAEA would maintain its own system of accountability, duplicating the system which the facility must maintain to account to its customers. If accountability to the IAEA to assure against diversion is no more precise than the accountability to customers, the IAEA need only supervise the plant accountability system to insure its integrity and exercise surveillance to exclude massive cheating. Such cheating would probably have to involve the facility operators, the customers, and the AEC inspectors. Substantial diversions short of a massive cheating system would show up in the company's accountability system.

NFS accountability to its customers is a far higher percentage than had ever been considered feasible at the time of other earlier studies of safeguards. It can be attained under existing technology only through certain procedures for averaging losses and gains from processing individual lots over a period of as long as a year, measurement of the recovered product on the premises, measurement of fissionable materials in the waste streams, and other techniques set forth in detail in the contracts between NFS and its customers.

The Argonne paper observed that the NFS experience suggested "a realistic and effective program with limited expenditures can be done by restricting the safeguard limits to those acknowledged by the plant accountability program. . . . It is again emphasized that the limits suggested, that is accountability alone, will to some extent be extended by virtue of the surveillance effort applied."[6] The paper proposed an independent determination of the accountability of safeguarded plutonium through independent sampling and analysis using "relatively sophisti-cated" apparatus that may include television systems, monitors, alarm devices, tamper-proof seals, laboratory facilities, and analytical equip-ment.

The paper further concluded that the program would not require much additional physical surveillance. The large number of observers would interfere with plant operations, result in severe personality conflicts be-tween the inspectorate and plant management, and create problems in finding a sufficient number of qualified inspectors. The increased cost of the additional assurance would pass the point of diminishing returns.

Verification of Isotope Separation Plants

The extension of IAEA inspection to isotope separation plants in-volves different problems. The United States proposal to the ENDC does not contemplate complete access to all parts of the plant, as in the case of chemical processing plants.

The system of verification for U–235 separation plants is described as follows:

(i) A U–235 separation plant capable of producing enriched U–235 can represent a potential for diversion or illegal production of significant amounts of fissionable material suitable for use in weapons. . . .

(ii) Inspection would involve: (1) Ground access at the perimeter of the process buildings, with continuous examination of the perimeters; (2) measurement of electrical power input to the plant; and (3) measurement of perimeter uranium input and declared product output, and uranium tails, for uranium content and U–235 content.

(iii) This inspection will permit an estimate of the U–235 production potential adequate at present to assure against diversions which would be significant relative to existing stocks.[7]

Fissionable materials suitable for use in atomic weapons are of three kinds: plutonium, uranium–233, and uranium–235. Plutonium and U–233 are produced in nuclear reactors and separated in chemical process-ing plants. Uranium–235, however, is an isotope of uranium which is separated in an isotope separation plant from the more abundant non-fissionable isotopes found in nature. The only process by which this is being done in quantity is by the gaseous diffusion process.

There are several reasons for not allowing complete access to gaseous diffusion plants. The danger of diversion of fissionable materials from an isotope separation plant may be less than from a chemical processing plant. This is true in part because of the precise measurements of plant production which can be made through observations at the perimeter and by measuring the use of electricity. Also, diversions would usually take place at the perimeters. Moreover, in isotope separation—unlike chemical processing—much technology is still secret.

The problem of monitoring and verifying production of U–235 isotopes at a gaseous diffusion plant has been studied for the U.S. AEC. These studies concluded that an inspection and verification system based on material accountability and physical security: (a) could detect significant amounts of unauthorized diversions of fissionable uranium; (b) would require two or three hundred people per plant (approximately 1,000 for the three U.S. plants), most of whom would be security and administrative personnel; (c) could not guarantee prevention of some diversion, one-half of one percent at best, or 10 percent or more under unfavorable assumptions; and (d) could *not* be effective without some access to areas within the plant perimeter.[8]

From the situation postulated in this study, these conclusions require modification. Under any production control agreement there is no way of accurately determining past production and thus no way of ascertaining stockpiles of states which have already undertaken production of fissionable material. Second, there is no known way at present of being positive that an undetected clandestine facility is not at work producing fissionable material.

These points are recognized in recent U.S. proposals which make no provision for monitoring or estimating stockpiles and which rely on existing national intelligence to learn of clandestine facilities. These considerations affect the evaluation of any verification system in a production plant. Since none of the prepared verification plans would be able to detect or prevent diversion from a nation's stockpiles, it does not appear necessary to determine accurately and continuously the inventory of fissionable material held at intermediary storage points or in process equipment within the production plant. Such inventories may properly be considered part of the national stockpile. The technical significance of this point is amplified below. Moreover, the possibility of clandestine production occurring within the production complex is no greater than the possibility of clandestine production at any other location.

Description of an Isotope Separation Plant (Gaseous Diffusion Process). Several features of a gaseous diffusion plant are pertinent to this discussion:

1. They are so expensive (over $1 billion each) that few exist in the world: 3 in the United States, 1 in the United Kingdom, 1 in the Soviet Union, 1 in France, and 1 in Communist China (which may be a different type of plant).

2. They are very large—thousands of acres of facilities at each site, hundreds of acres of process buildings, several miles of perimeter fence, hundreds of miles of process pipe, a thousand miles of copper tubing,

several thousand miles of wiring, and equipment or materiel crossing the site perimeter every minute or two around the clock.

3. They are very complex and process equipment is not directly accessible.

4. A large inventory of fissionable material is necessarily tied up in process and in intermediary storage. This inventory is not fixed, but varies slowly and in a complex manner. This makes it difficult to monitor the plant by simply balancing input against output at the perimeter.

5. The process involves classified national security information, disclosure of which to states not at present able to construct such plants could accelerate proliferation of the ability to produce atomic weapons.

The gaseous diffusion process consists of pumping large quantities of a gaseous uranium compound (UF_6) through thousands of porous diffusion barriers, each of which passes a slightly greater quantity of the smaller U–235 atoms than the larger, slower, non-fissionable isotopes. The process gas (UF_6) is fed through a cascade of diffusion barrier units. The gas stream divides, one part growing richer in U–235 as it passes through the barriers, the remaining part being removed and pumped in the opposite direction. The latter stream is discarded. This stream, depleted in U–235, is commonly known as "tails." A large number of diffusion stages through which the gas streams flow in opposite directions are combined to form a production cascade.

Parameters of an Inspection System. The best means of monitoring the production of such a plant with minimal intrusion would be to check all material entering and leaving the plant, analyze for U–235 where appropriate, and check the material balance for diversion. Electrical imput could also be monitored, since production of U–235 is roughly proportional to it.

However, studies made by the AEC claim that such a system would be ineffective and that an effective system would require a degree of intrusion which would compromise security information and interfere with plant operation. The assumptions underlying this conclusion are:

1. General access to the plant perimeter encompasses not only the production cascades but also several storage and handling operations whose contents cannot be determined from the perimeter.

2. The cascade is fed from the main feed point and at other points along the cascade corresponding to feed materials from reactor fuels or other sources whose U–235 content differs from the natural uranium in the main feed stream.

3. There are effluents other than top product and tails. Withdrawals are made at various enrichments for reactor fuel and other purposes. There are waste streams, and equipment is removed for repairs or other reasons, unavoidably taking uranium of various enrichments with it.

4. These multiple inputs and outputs must be monitored if production is to be known, and they continually keep the plant out of equilibrium so that a simple balance of output versus input cannot be made.

5. Electrical power fed into the plant perimeter is consumed by operations other than the production cascade and therefore is not representative of U–235 production.

This situation can be simplified by requiring that the production cascade be the only part of the facility that is monitored. Storage and handling facilities within the site boundaries would be treated separately in the same manner as similar facilities elsewhere. The actual location of the guarded perimeter in each particular plant would have to be established by detailed study of the facility. For example, the contaminated equipment facilities might have to be included within the perimeter to avoid revealing classified design information. This kind of accommodation to the physical realities of each plant should be possible without affecting the validity of the monitoring system.

It is suggested the following be monitored:

1. *Input Streams*—material flow, uranium, U–235—in (a) the main process feed (natural uranium); and (b) cascade side feeds (various enrichments).[9]

2. *Output Streams*—material flow, uranium, U–235—in (a) the top product ("fully enriched uranium"); (b) tails (fully depleted uranium") (c) cascade side withdrawals (various enrichments);[10] (d) miscellaneous waste streams; and (e) removed contaminated equipment.

3. *Electricity* consumption by the production cascade.

In addition to monitoring declared process streams entering and leaving the cascade and electricity consumption the inspection team would patrol the perimeter for packages arriving and leaving the area, undeclared process streams (e.g., underground), smuggling by personnel, and clandestine electrical input.

To make these input-versus-output measurements meaningful and to minimize the effects of changes in plant inventory or hold-up, the plant could be required to return to within a specified percent of input-equals-output within a specified time. To demonstrate good faith, material could be brought temporarily from stockpiles to compensate for unexpectedly large deviations in plant inventory.

Another indicator of intent to divert would be evidence that the plant was operating far from theoretically optimum conditions. This would show up in electricity consumption per unit of U–235 output, or it might be deduced from analyses of the sidestreams themselves.

Studies sponsored by the AEC have usually recommended verification systems based on those already developed for routine material accountability in facilities handling fissionable materials. Although much can be applied from experience with such systems, there are important differences in the objectives and operation of a system for providing daily routine accountability of fissionable material and a system for detecting deliberate and sizable diversion. These differences should be considered in comparing systems designed for the two purposes. An examination of procedures used by a business for routine bookkeeping and the procedures used by an investigating team looking for evidence of embezzlement are instructive.

In normal operations a discrepancy of fissionable materials represents a potential loss of money, whether it arises from a large amount of dilute solution inadvertently sent to waste storage tanks, a hidden bookkeeping error, or an accidental mixing of process fluids. These "losses" when added numerically do not constitute a quantity of divertible material capable of being converted into a weapon. Greater precision is required for routine control than for detection of significant diversion. A routine accountability system is relatively inflexible. It requires a large number of people to produce and analyze data with little room for innovation. The effectiveness of such a system can be analyzed statistically and the percentage of losses or discrepancies below the threshhold of detectability can be computed for various "confidence levels." Such an analysis is not valid for a diversion-inspection system. The essence of the latter is unpredictability with a capability of using new methods of analysis or new ways of looking at data. An imaginative divertor will probably be successful against a static detection system. Such an analysis would "prove" that no investigating team would have a reasonable chance of uncovering evidence of graft, embezzlement, or mismanagement. Yet one and two-man investigating teams in banks or businesses repeatedly turn up such evidence based on meager samples intelligently selected and evaluated.

One example of a useful technique will suffice for illustrative purposes. In a stable system one can work out methods for concealing diversion by falsifying records, biasing process meters, "doctoring" fluid streams, etc. Such techniques could produce a consistent set of data leading to the conclusion that no diversion was taking place. At this point, the inspectors could disturb the system and predict how the data would be affected. If a known quantity of uranium, with a known content of U–235, were fed into the system, all measured characteristics of the systems would be affected: the quantity and enrichment of all streams leaving the cascade, temperatures, pressures, and electrical power consumption. The exact weight and enrichment of the uranium introduced should be known only to the inspectorate. Even if the plant operators also knew the input, unless they had time and means to bias all the instruments and effluent streams, they could not prevent the erroneous reading from showing up. If the operators refused to permit "foreign" material to be fed to the cascade, a significant withdrawal from the cascade at an arbitrary point could serve the purpose. If the monitored variables did not respond predictably to the known perturbation, then the instrument readings would be suspect.

The considerable laboratory facilities and personnel of the government agency operating the plant would be utilized and spot checked, but not duplicated. There are simple techniques for independently checking instrument readings and chemical analyses. Samples of known uranium content can be submitted, occasional independent analyses can be made, "clamp-on" electrical meters can be used, and so on. Additional flexibility can be provided by occasionally using a different analytical technique or checking records or samples not usually verified. For example, if U–235 is usually checked by alpha-counters in a process stream, this could be "biased" by adding the correct quantity of another non-fissionable, alpha-emitting isotope. This would fool an alpha-counter, but it would not deceive a mass spectrometer.

Requirements for a System to Monitor Production of U–235 in a Gaseous Diffusion Plant. Noting the differences discussed above between a system for detecting diversion and one derived directly from normal materials accountability and physical security requirements, the following conclusions apply to the type of verification inspection system needed to support the type of production cutoff proposal contained in the U.S. paper ENDC/134:

The degree of perimeter inspection proposed in ENDC/134 for a gaseous diffusion plant could do an adequate job, recognizing the limitation of any inspection agreement in which stockpiles are not declared or monitored and clandestine facilities may escape detection. The perimeter must be defined so as to surround the production cascade to permit monitoring of all process streams entering and leaving the cascade. It must be permitted to analyze each process stream (including waste streams and removed equipment) for total uranium and U–235 when desired. It must be permitted to monitor electricity entering the production cascade. Plant production records should be available for inspection. If existing laboratory personnel and security personnel are utilized and not duplicated (as recommended herein), dozens of inspectors and security guards per plant, rather than hundreds, should suffice. This is less than fifty for the three U.S. plants and 100 to 150 for the entire world.

Flexibility in using different analytical techniques, examining different records, sampling new streams, or hooking up standardized instruments is essential to effective operation. The minimum predictability consistent with other requirements should be the goal.

Recognizing that the main objective of any cutoff agreement is to inhibit proliferation of atomic weapons among states not now having them, arrangements and procedures for verification at gaseous diffusion plants should be designed to prevent access to restricted data on gaseous diffusion technology. Facilities associated with a gaseous diffusion plant complex other than the production cascade itself should be considered outside the perimeter and thus part of the national fuel cycle. The fact that they are located near a gaseous diffusion plant is not fundamentally important to the verification process.

Inspection would be more effective if inspectors had limited access to the interior of plants to supplement and confirm their findings resulting from perimeter inspection. Even though the inspection system here proposed might be implemented without disclosing important secret technology, the inspection of isotope separation plants should be reciprocal rather than international, perhaps for the next ten years, to avoid proliferation through disclosure of technology to nationals of states not possessing facilities for isotope separation.

The development of gas centrifuge or other novel technology for isotope separation would not materially increase the problem of verification of declared facilities. The gas centrifuge facilities almost certainly would be smaller in size and therefore more numerous than gaseous diffusion plants. This would require a greater total number of inspectors, though fewer for each plant. The methods of inspection would be reciprocal and would be similar in principle to that used for gaseous diffusion installation. The major verification problem in connection with gas centrifuges is in detection of clandestine operations.

IAEA Inspection of Miscellaneous Facilities Handling Fissionable Materials

The "nuclear fuel cycle" is the term used to refer to the processes by which fissionable materials are converted from raw ores to nuclear fuels for weapons or for the production of electricity. Uranium ores processed in mines and mills emerge as "uranium concentrates." Up to this point, uranium cannot be used in atomic weapons. It then goes to feed preparation facilities which convert the concentrates to pure uranium metal or to uranium chemicals. These facilities may also process plutonium or uranium enriched by the fissionable isotope U–235. Since these materials may be used in bombs as well as in reactors the first necessity for inspection arises.

The pure metal or chemicals from the feed preparation facility are sent either to an isotope separation plant or to a reactor fuel fabrication facility. The former produces fissionable material and must be monitored as heretofore described. The latter presents an inspection problem similar to the feed preparation facility. These are both described below.

24

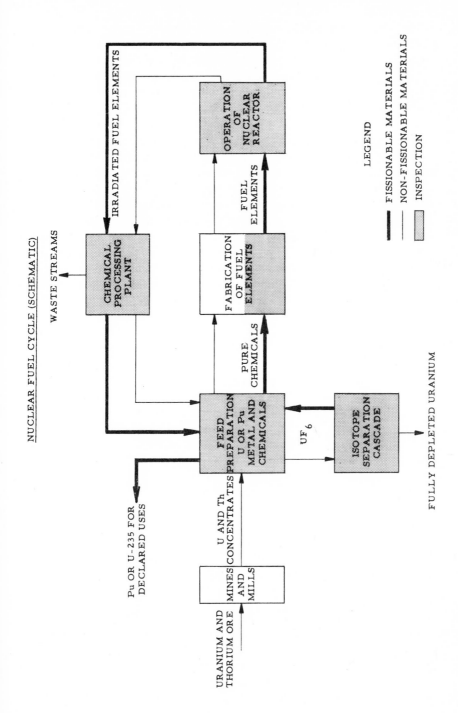

NUCLEAR FUEL CYCLE (SCHEMATIC)

The feed preparation facility may also produce weapons-grade plutonium and U–235 for such authorized non-weapons uses as peaceful nuclear explosions (the "Plowshare Program"), plutonium-consuming reactors, U–235-consuming reactors for research and naval nuclear propulsion, special research requirements, and certain foreign reactors. These products would be declared and the authorized end-uses would have to be verified.

The next step in the cycle is the nuclear reactor. Since reactors can produce weapons-grade plutonium by neutron bombardment of the naturally abundant non-fissionable isotope U–238, reactors must be monitored. The existing system operating under IAEA by which reactors are inspected to deter and detect any unauthorized diversion of fissionable material, and the measures to be taken to make the existing system adequate to verify a production cutoff, have been previously described.

The last link in the chain, which also has been discussed, is the chemical processing plant where fuel elements from the reactor are dissolved and uranium and plutonium are separated from waste products. From the chemical processing plant uranium and plutonium compounds are sent to the feed preparation facilities to repeat the cycle.

All of the above applies to uranium and its irradiation product, plutonium. The natural element thorium undergoes a similar cycle, although it is much less widely used at present. Thorium, like natural uranium, is not suitable for atomic bombs. However, after the concentrates are purified and fabricated into fuel elements, some of the thorium is converted under irradiation to the man-made uranium isotope U–233, which is fissionable and can be made into bombs. The process is analogous to the conversion of natural uranium into plutonium. The same principles and processes apply, and the same facilities would be used.

An important feature of the fuel cycle and the industrial-governmental complex which carries it out is its interdependence. Not only can a complete material balance be made and checked around any component of the cycle, but the entire national uranium and plutonium "economy" must balance. For example, the following equation must balance for quantities physically measurable on the site of a chemical processing plant or for any single tank of component within the plant:

Uranium entering = Uranium leaving + legitimate holdup or losses.

The same type of balance must apply to U–235, to plutonium, to thorium, to U–233, and to any other chemicals one may wish to check. If both the U–235 and the plutonium balanced, but the total uranium did not, or the nitrate ion did not, something would be taking place which is not being measured, and an investigation would be in order.

Independent of the above, there are other relationships which must check out. For example, for every pound of plutonium produced, a calculable quantity of U–238 is consumed. In addition, a predictable amount of heat is produced, and a known quantity of each of several hundred fission product isotopes is created. These can be checked. In the isotope separation plant each degree of separation is accomplished through the consumption of a roughly predictable amount of electricity and the discharge of a known amount of waste heat. These can also be checked. The major implication of this interdependence is that if one wished to divert clandestinely a fraction of any process stream at any part of the national fuel cycle complex and to conceal this diversion by false readings and false bookkeeping, he would find that he had affected, and would thus have to falsify, an ever-widening circle of meter readings and book entries at facilities all over the country. Many of these could easily be checked without interfering in the operation of the facility.

The U.S. proposal (ENDC/134, June 25, 1964) does not specifically provide for inspection of the feed preparation or fuel fabrication facilities, the transportation between the facilities, and storage associated with the system. These processes are carried out at several locations. In some cases part of the feed preparation processes are carried out at fuel element fabrication sites, which are sometimes located at reactor sites. As a case in point, production reactors at Hanford, Washington, have complete fuel fabrication facilities associated with them as well as complete chemical processing facilities. On the other hand, there are facilities which perform just part of one process, e.g., fabrication of small coated spheres from uranium oxide produced elsewhere.

The number of facilities in the United States other than reactors, isotope separation plants, and chemical processing plants which would require application of some safeguards is approximately as follows: eight producers of uranium for commercial use; eleven fabricators of uranium fuel, most of which is slightly enriched and not suitable for weapons use; nine organizations with an existing or planned capability for plutonium work; ten firms processing thorium, which cannot be used in bombs; and three firms working with the U–233 product of thorium which is weapons material. Since in some instances several processes are performed in a single facility, the total number of facility locations is no more than two or three dozen.

These facilities do not constitute a formidable total, especially when duplications are taken into account, and only a few of those listed are capable of handling material of high U–235 enrichment usable in weapons. Such facilities would be spot checked occasionally to ensure that a capacity for handling weapons-grade material had not been added.

The identification of facilities requiring inspection would thus have to be quite specific and perhaps would result in national decisions to limit the number of facilities handling fissionable materials usable in weapons. There might be other benefits from such a decision, e.g., consolidation of inspection requirements, closing down marginal facilities, etc.

One further aspect of monitoring the fissionable material cycle remains to be defined: declared, shutdown facilities. This category has been studied by AEC contractors who have operated such facilities and does not appear to present a serious problem.[11] Conventional security measures plus occasional spot checking would be adequate in view of the difficulty of starting up such a facility. In addition, a series of devices and procedures has been developed specifically for this problem: to "seal off" any device or part of a device which is supposed to remain shutdown or at a fixed setting. These devices and procedures have been used at the Hanford production reactor laboratories and also by the IAEA.

Thus, in the event of a cutoff policed by the IAEA, the following facilities or operations (in addition to reactors, chemical processing plants, and isotope separation plants) would require some verification: (1) shutdown production facilities; (2) fuel fabrication plants, in particular those where elements are fabricated utilizing highly enriched fissionable materials; (3) transportation of fuel elements to a reactor and from a reactor to chemical processing plants; (4) transportation of the plutonium and enriched uranium from chemical processing plants to other inspected facilities; and (5) facilities for storage of fissionable materials. The method of verification in each instance is relatively simple and involves no large personnel requirements.

Except for some facilities for storage of fissionable materials, an international system of inspection would seem preferable to reciprocal inspection primarily because of the large number of countries where such facilities would be located. The United States and the Soviet Union might insist on reciprocal inspection of facilities for storage of fissionable materials transferred by them from weapons stockpiles and also of closed down weapons production facilities.

IAEA Inspection to Detect Undeclared and Clandestine Facilities

The possible extension of the IAEA or any other international inspection control unit to detection of clandestine facilities gives rise to different and greater problems. The U.S. proposal to the ENDC suggests that:

The objective of an inspection of a suspected undeclared facility is to provide assurance that no U–235 separation plants, reactors, or chemical separation plants are in operation in violation of the agreement. That objective could be met by internal inspection of the facility or, in the case of a particularly sensitive facility, by appropriate external inspection procedures

28

such as environmental sampling, external observation of the structure, or the measurement of electrical power and other utilities within a radius of a few miles.[13]

The detection of a clandestine facility depends primarily upon intelligence data, which an international organization is unlikely to receive unless it is in a position to protect the source of the data. While this general problem exists under the cutoff, it is less of a problem than in other areas of arms control. The reason rests in the correlation of the fuel cycle phases. If the declared reactors are utilizing much more enriched fuel than is produced in the declared isotope separation plant, this would signify an undisclosed isotope separation plant. Similarly, if the declared reactors are using less than the full product of the declared isotope separation plant, this would signify that a portion of the isotope separation plant production was being utilized for other purposes. Similarly, there would be a direct relationship between the product coming from the chemical separation plants and the requirements for chemical separation of the declared reactors. The product of the chemical separation plant would either be placed in declared stockpiles or re-utilized in reactors with or without re-enrichment in isotope separation plants. A major violation detected in any of three phases of the fuel cycle would show up in the other phases. A major clandestine operation designed to escape from this nuclear accountability would almost surely involve a completely separate series of installations covering major phases of the fuel cycle. The agency verifying a cutoff will be certain to have available valuable sources of information concerning clandestine operations.

In conclusion, it is suggested that nearly any arrangement for detection and verification of clandestine operations in other areas of arms control would *a fortiori* be satisfactory in connection with a cutoff. Detection is an area in which it would be difficult to utilize the existing organization of the IAEA which has no system for maintaining classified information furnished to it, the prime requisite of an intelligence operation. The IAEA is planning to remedy this deficiency.

For the next five to ten years, clandestine operations outside the Soviet Union are unlikely to develop a significant nuclear weapons capability. During this same period, clandestine operations in the Soviet Union would probably not vitally affect the weapons capability of the Soviet Union vis-à-vis the West in view of the size of existing stockpiles.

Verification of the Cutoff by the IAEA

It was never contemplated that the IAEA during the early years of its existence would establish a safeguards system permitting it to carry out all its authorized functions in the field of safeguards.[14] The Report of the Preparatory Commission stated that "the safeguard procedure should keep pace with the development of the Agency's activities, starting with problems relating to the transport and storage of source and special fissionable materials and extending to the use of these materials in Agency-sponsored projects and to their subsequent treatment."[15]

Twenty-nine states have agreed to permit IAEA inspection of some seventy-five installations. None of these states, with the exception of the United States and the United Kingdom, which permit IAEA inspection of a limited number of facilities, has isotope separation plants or chemical processing plants. The portions of the nuclear fuel cycle to which the IAEA inspection system theoretically applies at present are transportation from port of entry to the reactor site, the utilization of the material in the reactors, arrangements to ensure that the material will not be diverted during the chemical processing, and storage of the recovered product.

The most complex of these would be the arrangements to ensure that the materials were not diverted during chemical processing. The Agency's approach to this problem, with one exception, has been tentative. Under the revised safeguards system adopted on February 25, 1965, the safeguards are suspended for irradiated fuel transferred for the purpose of reprocessing, and an equivalent amount of U–235 as determined by the Agency is substituted temporarily.[16] Upon completion of the reprocessing, the estimated amount of plutonium product is substituted for part of the U–235. This device, for the present, eliminates chemical processing from the inspection system of the IAEA.

The transportation of nuclear materials from the port of entry to the reactor site is also eliminated from the present inspection system of the IAEA. On an IAEA project the inspection system starts with a specified amount of materials delivered to the reactor by the IAEA. In the case of a reactor where the United States or another state furnishes the materials, the inspection system begins with the declaration of materials placed in the reactor pursuant to U.S. agreement. In view of the elimination of chemical processing from the system there is no reason to inspect transportation from the reactor to the chemical processing plant or from the chemical processing plant to the storage facility. The problem of the transfer of fissionable materials from a storage facility to a nuclear reactor is not dealt with under present IAEA regulations. For the present, IAEA inspection is confined to reactors and storage facilities plus a limited inspection of one chemical processing plant in the United States to verify the processing of spent fuels from a reactor already subject to IAEA inspection. An agency verifying the cutoff in states with complete nuclear installations such as the United States and the Soviet Union would have to consider the following additional activities: (1) milling and processing facilities for conversion of natural uranium into forms required for reactors, (2) isotope separation plants, (3) fuel fabrication plants, (4) chemical processing plants, (5) transportation from one plant to another at all stages of the fuel cycle, and (6) shut down production facilities.

While these additional areas of verification will require a staff many times larger than the few inspectors required for the present verification operations of the IAEA, several factors would tend to reduce the size of the required staff. The IAEA, in addition to its inspectors, has a technical staff to analyze reports and ensure accurate accountability of Agency-safeguarded material. The complexity of this task should not increase proportionately with the amount of materials. In some respects the task will be simplified by virtue of its universality. Moreover, precision in accountability might be less under a cutoff. In states with advanced development in the nuclear field, the facilities requiring verification tend to be large but few in number and therefore easier to inspect. The IAEA has one verification function which would not be required in a cutoff—assuring that scientific information developed by a state through an Agency project is made available to the Agency.

An Organization to Verify a Halt in Production Of Fissionable Materials For Weapons Purposes. Table 1–1 lists the number of sites in each geographic region (as of 1965) which might have to be visited by inspectors. The numbers are approximate, since some listed facilities share one site and other facilities may exist which were not accounted for. The shutdown of some facilities prior to the invitation to inspect is also assumed, e.g., nearly obsolete facilities or those dealing primarily with weapons materials, such as the chemical processing plants in Hanford and Savannah River. As an indication of possible growth rate, the number of power reactors expected by 1975 is tabulated. Other facilities would be expected to increase correspondingly except perhaps for research reactors which might grow rather more slowly.

As a basis for estimating the total number of inspectors needed, the table has been compiled on the basis of: (a) one inspector for each two or three power reactor sites, (b) one inspector for each ten research reactor sites, (c) six inspectors for each chemical processing plant, (d) six inspectors for each isotope separation plant, (e) two inspectors for each plutonium production reactor; and, (f) one inspector for each two miscellaneous fuel handling facilities.

In addition, the following factors were considered desirable: (a) no fewer than three inspectors in any one geographic region, (b) three-man teams available for power reactor inspections, (c) residence at each chemical processing plant of the six inspectors assigned to it, (d) residence at each isotope separation plant of the six inspectors assigned to it, (e) rotation of inspectors among the various types of inspection teams, and (f) rotation of inspectors between the field and headquarters.

These criteria lead to a reasonable approximation of total personnel in the inspectorate. The totals are as follows:

North American Region	85
South American Region	3
Western European Region	69
U.S.S.R. and Eastern European Region	29
Middle East and African Region	3
Far East and Oceania Region	21
	210
Inspectors at Headquarters (evaluation, training, rotation, etc.)	50
Total inspectors (based on 1965 facilities)	260

This total might double by 1975. It would seem feasible to hold the number to six or seven hundred.

The Inspector General directs the present IAEA inspection organization. Some services and support now supplied to the entire agency by the Deputy Director for Administration would continue to be drawn from that office. Other services peculiar to the inspection function such as in-service training and recruitment of professional personnel would be done by the inspectorate.

Based on 600 inspectors, the following approximate numbers of supporting personnel might be required:

Inspectors (HQ and field)	600	
Analysts, statisticians	60	
Foreign affairs experts	40	
Administrative officers	100	
Clerical and other non-professionals	240	(based on 30% of above)
Total	1040	

This total does not include security guards at certain facilities, where specific arrangements would be made in each case, perhaps on a reciprocal basis. The geographical distribution of personnel might be as shown in Table 1–2. The numbers and distribution of personnel shown in Tables 1–1 and 1–2 are not intended as precise predictions but merely to indicate the scope of the problem.

TABLE 1–1. Inspection Sites and Inspectors

	Power Reactors		Research Reactors	Chemical Processing Plants	Isotope Separation	Plutonium Production	Misc. Facilities	Totals
	1965	[1975]						
North	15	[70]	120	5	3	2	30	
America	(6)		(12)	(30)	(18)	(4)	(15)	(85)
South	0	[3]	3	0	0	0	0	
America			(3)					(3)
Western	19	[60]	87	5	2	2	10	
Europe	(9)		(9)	(30)	(12)	(4)	(5)	(69)
U.S.S.R. and	4	[10]	25	2	1	1	5	
Eastern Europe	(3)		(3)	(12)	(6)	(2)	(3)	(29)
Mid-East and	0	[2]	6	0	0	0	2	
Africa			(1)				(2)	(3)
Far East and	5	[25]	13	1	1	1	3	
Oceania	(3)		(1)	(6)	(6)	(2)	(3)	(21)
Total Sites	43	[170]	254	13	7	6	50	
Total Inspectors	(21)		(29)	(78)	(42)	(12)	(28)	(210)

NOTE: Numbers of Inspectors are in parentheses. In addition to the field inspectors, there would be about 50 inspectors at headquarters for evaluation, training, rotation, etc.

SOURCE: Compiled from IAEA reports and other data.

TABLE 1–2. Approximate Geographic Distribution of Inspectorate Personnel

Region	Totals	Inspectors	Analysts, Data Handlers	Foreign Affairs Experts	Admin. Officers	Non-Prof. Support
Headquarters	361	137	44	28	68	84
North America	266	188	5	3	10	60
South America	16	8	1	1	2	4
Western Europe	219	150	5	3	10	51
U.S.S.R. and East Europe	92	63	2	2	4	21
Middle East and Africa	16	8	1	1	2	4
Far East and Oceania	70	46	2	2	4	16
Totals	1,040	600	60	40	100	240

Possible Changes in the Authority of the IAEA. The safeguards functions of the Agency, set forth in Article III.A(5), are:

To establish and administer safeguards designed to ensure that special fissionable and other materials, services, equipment, facilities, and information made available by the Agency or at its request or under its supervision or control are not used in such a way as to further any military purpose; and to apply safeguards, at the request of the parties, to any bilateral or multilateral arrangement, or at the request of a State, to any of that State's activities in the field of atomic energy.

It should first be noted that this provision does not require a state to agree to safeguards provisions through its adherence to the Agency Statute. The safeguards become applicable to a state if it applies for Agency assistance or, in the alternative, if it requests the Agency to apply its safeguards system either to its own activities or to activities resulting from bilateral or multilateral arrangements. Since neither the Soviet Union nor the United States would be seeking assistance from the Agency, they would be subject to the Agency system of safeguards only at their own request. Doubtless for this reason the Soviet Union was ready to approve a more extensive system of safeguards than it would have sanctioned within its own boundaries.

When a state becomes subject to the IAEA safeguards system, the statutory authority seems adequate to ensure against diversion of fissionable materials.[17] The sections of the IAEA responsible for the development and administration of safeguards, i.e., the Subcommittee of the Board of Governors and the Inspector General, have not found themselves hampered by provisions of the Statute. The question has been whether the IAEA will as a matter of policy utilize its existing authority rather than whether it would require additional authority.

However, the Statute has no provision similar to Article 2(6) of the United Nations Charter, "that states which are not Members of the United Nations act in accordance with these Principles so far as may be necessary for the maintenance of international peace and security." If a state does not voluntarily submit to the IAEA system, the IAEA has no way of assuring its observance of a cutoff. Presumably the United States and the Soviet Union, if they agreed on a cutoff, would voluntarily submit to the IAEA safeguards system.

If it became necessary to enforce the safeguards system all over the world, it might be necessary to amend the IAEA Statute or establish an International Disarmament Organization by a separate treaty to assume the responsibility for verifying the cutoff. The latter course might be easier to achieve than the former. The nuclear powers would be likely to insist that if IAEA obtains greatly increased authority the nuclear powers would require greater control over the Board of Governors.

The pressures in IAEA tend to diminish rather than increase the role of the great powers.

If immediate minor amendments of the Statute were required to permit the IAEA to verify a cutoff, such amendments should be easy to obtain once a cutoff had been agreed upon.

Possible Changes in Organizational and Personnel Patterns of the IAEA. The IAEA organization would have to be supplemented if it were expanded to verify a cutoff. It would be necessary to establish regional and, in some instances, country headquarters. A group or section in the Vienna headquarters of IAEA to deal with the problem of clandestine facilities should be created and should collect information obtained by the Agency itself and information furnished through national intelligence channels. This in turn would require the development of a security system to assure the protection of intelligence sources.

The IAEA would have to expand its system of liaison with member states to work out arrangements for seconding personnel. The problems of obtaining specialized personnel for the safeguards program are such that the Inspector General should have his own personnel section separate from the IAEA Office of Personnel. Moreover, the IAEA would have to establish a headquarters staff to provide the in-service training necessary for continuity of a large-scale operation.

With these additional organizational requirements, the verification of a cutoff by the IAEA would in general only require expansion of its existing arrangements. With regard to personnel increments, the number of inspectors should be increased at the outset of a cutoff to 400 and ultimately to 700. These numbers include inspection of all facilities and other activities related to the cutoff.

Approximately 25 percent of the inspectors would not be engaged in actual inspections and would be assigned to other functions for which they were qualified. These functions would include: the training program, along with training at the Austrian reactor at Seibersdorf and the IAEA laboratory in Seibersdorf as well as the central headquarters and regional offices of IAEA where a portion of the staff would require the same qualifications as the inspectors.

While the IAEA Statute provides in theory for an international service, both the specific terms of the Statute and the nature of IAEA functions assure a staffing pattern quite different from that of most U.N. specialized agencies. The Statute contemplates a high proportion of personnel from the nuclear powers, including the Soviet Union. For practical purposes this eliminates recruitment through competitive examinations. All appointments of officer personnel to date have been "limited" appointments, not exceeding two years, rather than indefinite appointments. This conforms to the statutory injunction that the permanent staff be kept to a minimum. Another factor leading to short appointments was the policy of the new Director General that no important appointees have tenure extending more than six months past the period of his own appointment.

The analysts and statisticians, the foreign affairs experts, and the miscellaneous officer staff that would be required to permit the IAEA to assume the functions of verifying a cutoff are neither so numerous nor require such unique talents that their recruitment would present a major problem. Obtaining the inspectors would pose some problems both because of the larger number required and because of the necessity for specialized skills and training.

It was generally agreed not only by the administrative officers of IAEA but top administrative personnel of other U.N. specialized agencies that the IAEA inspection corps could not maintain its character as an international verification organ if more than 40 percent of the inspectors came from the United States, the United Kingdom, and the Soviet Union.

At present, practically all officer personnel of IAEA are seconded to the IAEA by its members. Each inspector must be approved by the Board of Governors. Inspectors are generally appointed for a two-year term.

The major positions in the IAEA tend to be allocated among states with the result that when the term of an incumbent is completed, the successor comes from the same state. Promotions are virtually impossible. These weaknesses in the personnel program limit the expansion capabilities of the IAEA to a greater degree than the shortage of qualified personnel. Fundamental changes in personnel policy seem essential, therefore, if the IAEA is to assume broader functions.

Because a large proportion of personnel from communist states will be part of the verification organization, it seems likely that most personnel including inspectors will be seconded to the IAEA by states and that terms of appointment will be for a specified number of years. However, the terms should be for five years or more rather than for two years. This would permit personnel to acquire the necessary expertise in their functions. If they remain for five years, their rights in the U.N. pension fund will become established and they would have at least a theoretical alternative to returning to their states. This possibility would afford some incentive to act in the interests of the international community rather than as agents of their states of origin. The Director General should have the discretion to retain the services of inspectors beyond their terms of appointment even without the consent of the national government concerned.

The establishment of an extensive in-service training program would be essential. While appointees to positions as inspectors would be certain to have training in reactor technology, they would not be likely to have experience with the engineering, administrative, and legal problems involved in inspections. In-service training should make it possible for the new appointees to assume their responsibilities earlier than would otherwise be possible.

The IAEA lacks specialists in technical areas such as waste disposal. Initially, such specialists would probably have to be obtained for short assignments without regard to the usual personnel procedures. This is an infrequent problem for each field of specialization and should not be too difficult to solve.

IAEA officials have suggested that individual positions should not, as at present, be allotted by states. The existing practice raises havoc with any system of promotions through merit, since the immediate superior of a deserving employee will ordinarily come from a different state. Instead, the Director General should assure each state of its proper quota of the total positions. If the verification machinery becomes larger than the rest of the IAEA, it would seem preferable to have separate liaison arrangements between the Inspector General and the member states. This is one of the prime reasons for suggesting a separate personnel office for the Inspector General.

Financing IAEA Safeguards. Article XIV of the Agency statute raises problems concerning the financing of Agency safeguards which merit detailed consideration. This article divides IAEA expenses into two categories: administrative expenses and other expenses. The article specifically requires that the costs of administering the safeguards system be deemed administrative expenses.

Expenses of administering safeguards undertaken "at the request of a state" with respect to any of that state's activities were not specifically included among the expenses that must be deemed administrative expenses. This makes it possible for the United States, the United Kingdom, the Soviet Union, and any other states not recipients of assistance either from the Agency or from other states to finance the safeguards system themselves.

For the next ten years most of the expenses of the safeguards system could be allocated to the nuclear powers with lesser amounts allocated to states which are parties to bilateral or multilateral arrangements. However in the 1975–80 period, the cost of administering safeguards in states other than the present nuclear powers would be so great that if the Statute were not interpreted to provide sufficient flexibility, it should be amended to provide a different method of financing.

Reciprocal Inspection Within IAEA System. Reciprocal inspection of isotope processing facilities and closed down production facilities has been indicated as the appropriate system. The isotope separation facilities would be in the United States, United Kingdom, Soviet Union, and possibly France and Communist China. Reciprocal inspection of isotope separation facilities is necessary because much of the technology is secret. Dissemination of this knowledge even to the international inspectorate might be inconsistent with a prime objective of the cutoff—to prevent nuclear proliferation. The closed down production facilities would be in the United States, the Soviet Union, and possibly the United Kingdom. International inspection of closed down production facilities might furnish information about past production of enriched uranium and plutonium, an area outside the scope of a cutoff.

The IAEA Statute does not prevent the delegation of some of the verification functions to groups operating on a reciprocal basis. Since any responsibility of the IAEA to verify isotope separation plants or closed down production facilities would arise as a result of agreements with states for such verification, the agreement could specify the method of verification. However, the IAEA would not be responsible for the acts or omissions of personnel not subject to its control.

Inspection of the closed down facilities to see that they remain closed would be a comparatively simple task. The inspectors could report compliance or violation to their national governments, which presumably would communicate violations to the IAEA. Inspection of isotope separation facilities would require direct communication from the inspectors of the statistical data, which would be part of the worldwide accountability system established at the IAEA headquarters. It would be feasible for the IAEA regional headquarters to furnish administrative services to the reciprocal inspectors, and it might even be possible to include the reciprocal inspectors in the status agreements negotiated between the IAEA and the countries where inspections take place.

Procedures Governing Inspections. The IAEA system is set forth in four documents not wholly consistent with each other.[18] In addition, the inspections are governed by the agreements providing for IAEA inspection in the specific state. These are usually trilateral agreements between the IAEA, the state where the facility is located, and the state responsible for furnishing the nuclear materials and assistance (the United States or the United Kingdom). It should be noted that these agreements may not be identical even for a single state. For example, the agreement providing for inspection of Japanese facilities receiving assistance from the United Kingdom differs from the agreement relating to the facilities assisted by the United States.

The procedures required to establish a system of IAEA inspection in a state are extremely complex and time consuming. In the case of inspection of U.S.-assisted facilities located in Japan, seven steps preceded the initial inspection: (a) trilateral negotiations between the IAEA, the United States, and Japan; (b) Board of Governors approval of the Trilateral Agreement; (c) signature of the Agreement; (d) acceptance by the IAEA of materials inventory and consequent bringing of the Agreement into force; (e) pre-operational visits by IAEA personnel; (f) agreement between the IAEA and Japan on designation of inspectors; and (g) agreement between the IAEA and Japan on detailed procedures.

Ten months elapsed between the time that the United States and Japan first announced their intention to utilize IAEA verification and the IAEA personnel were first brought into the negotiations.

The Inspector General has made specific suggestions to reduce the number of steps and to permit some to be carried on simultaneously. However, the problem of ensuring that verification proceed with minimal friction between the IAEA and the states to be inspected can be met only through a grant of broad authority to the IAEA by agreement or General Conference action to set up detailed procedures and regulations and the promulgation of regulations covering as many specific situations as possible.[19]

Utilizing the IAEA to Verify the Cutoff. The chief advantage of utilizing the IAEA as the agency to verify a cutoff is that it already has an established safeguards system inspecting reactors. The IAEA has developed an effective medium for technical discussion of verification problems in a forum that includes all nuclear powers except Communist China. With great effort the IAEA has developed procedures for access by the inspectors to the facilities, for carrying out certain types of inspection, and for reporting results. While some of the existing procedures are cumbersome and could be improved, their use was necessary before the imperfections became apparent. On the basis of experience the small inspection staff has done precise and specific planning of its requirements to undertake broader functions. A substitute agency would take at least three years to reach the point already attained by the IAEA.

The Statute gives the IAEA adequate authority to assume the functions of verifying a cutoff under existing conditions. The considerable administrative changes would be no more difficult to obtain in the IAEA than to establish a new agency. The financing of verification within the territories of the nuclear powers could be obtained by agreement between the IAEA and the great powers. Financing of verification elsewhere would probably be feasible for several years through an enlarged IAEA administrative budget.

As the quantities of fissionable materials in the program of peaceful uses of the atom increase the ratio of the amounts of such materials to materials in weapons stockpiles will also increase. Sometime in the late seventies several major changes in the IAEA Statute may become essential, since: (1) it is improbable that the major nuclear powers would entrust the direction of the verification program to the present Board of Governors, (2) the verification organ might require types of sanctions exceeding the extremely limited sanctions available under the present Agency Statute, (3) in the event a state not acceding to the cutoff began to develop a vast weapons capability the responses might require types of international action beyond those comprehended in the IAEA Statute, and (4) the financing of a vast verification program might be hampered if the provisions of the present IAEA Statute were construed too inflexibly.

When that point is reached, it would probably be more satisfactory to set up a new agency than to attempt to revise the IAEA. If the cutoff were not the only measure of arms control requiring international verification, it might be desirable to include all verification systems under a newly created agency.

Some have contended that the IAEA is more acceptable as a verification agency because states are eager to obtain the benefits mainly without cost of the remainder of its programs. It is suggested that this is not a valid argument. In the event of a cutoff, the safeguards would overshadow the other functions.

It might be supposed that the highest degree of technical precision would be the proper objective for an inspection system monitoring a production cutoff, with inspection teams totaling 10,000 or even 45,000. However, this is not necessarily the case.

The military potential of existing stockpiles which are assumed to be unaffected by the cutoff agreement is so large that even a substantial diversion of anticipated production for peaceful purposes during the next ten years would not increase them appreciably. Therefore, a system of high technical effectiveness would not provide significantly greater protection against atomic destruction by the nuclear powers than a system of only modest capability, e.g., 90 percent assurance that no more than 10 percent of the declared production is diverted. Yet even a modest system would help prevent the proliferation of weapons to non-atomic nations. Given existing stockpiles, a small undetected diversion could not cause the gross upset of world stability that was envisioned in the days when only a few such weapons existed.

No inspection system can be technically perfect. As flaws in the technical effectiveness of the control system were uncovered, increasingly intrusive means would have to be devised to eliminate them. It would become apparent to political leaders and the public alike that each loophole closed would suggest the possibility of other loopholes. The impracticability of providing a "fool-proof" system would soon become clear. The resulting disillusionment could become a serious handicap to consideration of other arms control measures.

If an inspection system were established with a mandate for assuring that a certain low and precise level of diversion is not exceeded, an inherent source of friction would be created *ipso facto*. The more familiar the inspection teams become with the magnitude and uncertainties of their assigned tasks, the more they could be expected to inform the respective states of their suspicions and concern, while at the same time applying more stringent measures to reduce the uncertainties. These actions would tend to increase, rather than decrease, international tensions.

The more a system is "improved" to accomplish a narrowly-defined technical objective, the less flexibility it has for coping with technical and political changes. Flexibility might turn out to be the most important attribute of an inspection system. An international inspection organization would facilitate further moves in the right direction: a system aimed at too narrow an objective could be not only harmful in itself, but could also increase the possibility of atomic destruction.

In view of these discouraging arguments, it is pertinent to ask whether any kind of inspection organization could be developed which might have value, and, if so, to attempt to define the characteristics it should have and the criteria by which it should be judged.

First, we should ask whether any international inspection system can be justified solely on its own merits. Can the decreased probability of atomic destruction produced by such a system be great enough to justify its cost? With the large uninspected weapons stockpiles which exist, an inspection system cannot, by itself, eliminate atomic weapons of the present nuclear powers. Unlike weapons test cessation, which offered an immediate halt to the buildup of fallout, a production cutoff offers no dramatic, immediate, and direct benefit.

However, our standard of comparison should not be an abstract ideal, but rather the existing condition of no controls at all. Any major improvement in this situation must be judged in that light.

How can we define the objectives of a system whose stated technical mission must not be pursued unreservedly? What is its real purpose? Perhaps we can learn from some similar examples. Let us consider a problem posed by the U.S. Atomic Energy Act of 1954: to establish a system and an organization for inspection of all uses of nuclear materials which might create a public hazard and to monitor operations so that no undue hazard is in fact created. Here is a requirement whose technical dimensions are commensurate with the international inspection problem, and whose political aspects, though different, are not trivial. The dangers of an overly technical approach in this case parallel those cited for the cutoff inspection problem. Yet it was concluded that a system of modest technical capability, sensitive to political and economic realities, could serve a useful function. Does it guarantee that no unsafe operations will occur? Hardly. Yet it provides a framework for sufficiently flexible governmental controls to be passed to the states as the time becomes appropriate and to be modified in other ways as technical and political requirements emerge. A mechanism has been established, regulation is being practiced, and an excellent safety record has been achieved. The problem has now been reduced to one of drawing on a growing body of precedents and improving an existing mechanism.

Since the building of confidence is an objective of any new inspection system, it is important not to set unattainable goals. A modestly effective inspection system would provide a reasonable degree of national security. We may surmise from experience in technical developments that lowering requirements often simplifies the system in question, e.g., developing a ship to travel 30 knots is a qualitatively different and far less difficult task than developing a 40-knot ship.

CONCLUSION

A verification organization of reasonable size stemming from the present IAEA could for the next decade furnish reasonable assurance against significant violations of an agreement to devote all future production of fissionable materials to non-weapons uses. While such assurance would not be airtight, it could afford a structure which would enhance that assurance, especially in comparison to the existing situation of no agreement and no verification. To be effective, however, production accountability, which is the main basis for such assurance, would depend upon establishment of orderly procedures in the near future before the proliferation of fissionable materials reaches a stage where no verification system could be effective. Just as the Baruch proposals became outdated by 1953, the present non-proliferation treaty proposals will become obsolete in the near future unless we have moved a long distance toward their acceptance and implementation by all states. Therefore, an organization of reasonable size, which the Soviet Union might be willing to accept at this time and which could give considerable assurance against major violations, is necessary. The successful operation of such an organization would be the major impetus for developing a system to deal adequately with the vastly more complex situation which will exist when the quantity of fissionable materials multiplies manyfold.

GOMULKA PROPOSALS AND RAPACKI PLAN

The Rapacki Plan, advanced by the Polish Foreign Minister, Adam Rapacki, has undergone several revisions since it was first set forth in October 1957. The last version, tabled on March 28, 1962, at the ENDC in Geneva, provided for a ban on the production, stockpiling, and deployment of equipment and facilities for nuclear weapons and delivery vehicles. The ban would be binding on the Federal Republic of Germany (FRG), the German Democratic Republic (GDR), Czechoslovakia, and Poland, as well as on the four nuclear powers maintaining forces on the territories of these countries. The nuclear powers would undertake not to transfer nuclear weapons to any of the four Central European countries or to use nuclear weapons against them. The states concerned would establish an effective verification system to ensure implementation of the obligations assumed.

The Gomulka Proposals constituted a less complicated scheme intended to be a partial step towards realization of the Rapacki Plan. Originally presented in a speech by the First Secretary of the Polish United Workers Party, Wladyslaw Gomulka, on December 28, 1963, the Gomulka Proposals were submitted formally to the governments concerned on February 29, 1964, in the form of a "Memorandum on the Freezing of Nuclear and Thermonuclear Armaments in Central Europe." The Proposals called for a freeze of the existing nuclear *status quo* in the territories of the aforementioned four Central European countries. The governments maintaining armed forces on these territories (including West Berlin) would undertake not to produce, introduce, import, or transfer to other parties in the area or to accept from other parties in the area nuclear or thermonuclear weapons. An "appropriate system" of supervision and safeguards would be initiated.

The Gomulka Proposals (G Plan) and the Rapacki Plan (R Plan) are discussed below solely in the light of problems they may pose for effective verification and for the international organization of such verification. Military and political implications are not examined. The Gomulka Proposals, being the most recent and the more limited, are discussed first.

THE GOMULKA PROPOSALS

The Gomulka Proposals provide for a freeze of the quantity of weapons and, impliedly, the national control over these weapons, in prohibiting their "transfer to, or acquisition from, other parties."[1] The freeze on delivery vehicles, which figures prominently in the R Plan, was dropped entirely in the G Plan. A freeze on vehicles would serve the purposes of a quantitative freeze, supplement the transfer freeze, and would be easier to supervise because the vehicles are larger in size. Its omission may be indicative of Polish indifference to, or neglect of, supervision problems.

The "Quantitative Freeze"

The G Plan proceeds from the premise that the quantity of nuclear weapons in the area can be increased either through production, including the assembly of such weapons within the area, or by the introduction of nuclear weapons from outside. Article III calls on the parties to undertake two types of commitments (apart from the issue of transfer): first, not to produce nuclear weapons inside the area (the production cutoff); and second, not to "introduce or to import" them into the area.

Import may be understood to mean only the kind of operation that would fall under commercial import controls or restrictions. But when weapons are involved, they can also be "introduced" by military forces entering the country and bringing the weapons over the border as part of redeployment of forces or maneuvers. When discussing verification, this military type of "introduction" into the area deserves special attention, for it could place obstacles in the way of effective verification.

Article IV calls for the supervision of a production cutoff, defined as the termination of the "production of weapons in plants which are or could be used for such production." If this contemplates a freeze on the production of fissionable materials for weapons purposes, it is verifiable. If it also includes a freeze on the plants that manufacture the weapon itself and insert the fissionable material into the weapon, a serious verification obstacle would be created. It should be pointed out that if all production of fissionable material were safeguarded, there could be no nuclear weapons produced from such materials.

Since the Plan does not provide for a qualitative freeze, there is, logically, no mention of plants "producing" weapons improvements, such as laboratories or testing facilities. But if the Plan were intended to exclude from the import prohibition items serving as replacement, the quality issue could hardly be ignored. It can be argued that the main issue of replacement for nuclear weapons does not arise because no nuclear weapons will be used except in war, when the agreement would be terminated in any case. However, if replacement did occur, consideration would be required of the characteristics of weapons imported for replacement.

The supervision of imports at the points of entry listed in Article IV would not cover all imports because the required inspection of all regular shipments could paralyze border traffic. Warheads could be brought into the area along portions of the seacoast where there are no ports, or by planes and helicopters landing outside of airports. If small enough, warheads might even be carried across borders without using railways or roads. Whether such "smuggling" would need to be detected would depend on the degree of perfection required of the supervision system.

The Transfer or Control Freeze

This second type of freeze, mentioned in Article III, obliges the parties "not to transfer to other parties in the area or to accept from other parties in the area the aforementioned nuclear and thermonuclear weapons." What is to be included under the term "transfer" requires clarification. One may assume that the purpose is to prevent the dissemination of nuclear weapons from powers possessing them to non-nuclear powers in the area. But this calls for an agreed definition of what is to be understood by "possession" of such weapons or by what the G Plan calls "having them at one's disposal."

Three cases of transfer should be distinguished. If they are all to be included, the problem of supervision becomes exceedingly difficult if not impracticable; if one or two of them are excluded, dissemination remains possible.

First, nuclear weapons can be transferred physically by moving them within or into the area from locations under the sole control of an outside nuclear power to a location in which a country within the area would be able to use them at will.

Because there are nuclear weapons at present stockpiled within the Western part of the area—and perhaps in the Eastern part also—this type of physical transfer would call for supervision on all routes linking nuclear installations controlled by an outside power, such as American stockpiles of warheads or rocket bases, with territory under the authority of the host country. If it recognized the problem, the Polish Government must have had special reason to be silent about the inclusion of such routes of communication which would be essential to any effective transfer supervision. It may have feared negative Western reactions to a control system so implicitly comprehensive.

Second, transfer can also take place if the term is understood in a wider sense: dissemination or transfer could be said to occur whenever a non-nuclear country gains independent control of nuclear weapons, even if they are not taken into its physical possession. The FRG, for example, could then be said to gain "disposal" of nuclear weapons if German military personnel were put in charge of them even though the weapons were not separated physically from their American stockpiles or bases.

Here supervision of a transfer freeze would have to extend to the verification of the nationality of the men and officers placed in charge of the weapons. In that case, supervision would require access to information concerning the nationality of the personnel serving at all nuclear establishments in the area whether controlled by the host country or an outside power.

The third mode of transfer raises even more delicate and controversial questions. If the Soviet view on the NATO multilateral force as a form of alleged dissemination is accepted by the authors of the G Plan, then "transfer" of control from the United States to a joint allied command that included a non-nuclear country of the area would represent a transfer in the sense of the control freeze, and would have to be subjected to supervision.

Another form of joint control takes the form of the "two-key system." Even if the Soviet Union did not regard the system in which the Federal Republic of Germany holds one key as a form of dissemination, it would presumably consider a transformation into a one-key system, with the Federal Republic of Germany retaining the only key as a transfer of control of the kind prohibited by the G Plan. In order to be able to detect such a transfer, continuous observation would have to disclose whether the nuclear country which held the second key, was able to veto use of the weapons in question. This would be a difficult task in any circumstances, posing ticklish problems of secrecy, including the disclosure of supervision of arrangements at present withheld even from allied and domestic publics.

Supervision Under the G Plan

Much of what is known about verification of a nuclear cutoff is applicable to a freeze in the Central European area. To the extent that either the particular area or the special provisions of the G Plan introduce no peculiarities, the previous study on the international organizational arrangements for a verified agreement to halt production of fissionable materials for weapons purposes should be consulted. There are, however, some significant peculiarities in the G Plan. The following discussion will focus upon these and on the problems they pose.

Interest in the Proposed Freeze. The interest of the parties in a freeze agreement and its fulfillment bears directly on the degree of effectiveness and intensity of the supervision they may be expected to demand. The interest of Poland and Czechoslovakia (probably shared by the Soviet Union) in a nuclear freeze in Central Europe can be assumed to be great, since it would assure these states of the continued non-nuclearization of the FRG. The Western states involved in the Plan have shown no such interest in the freeze, not to mention denuclearization of the area, but have instead, according to various press accounts, repeatedly indicated that they regard the idea as harmful to their security interests.

There are two reasons for these contrasting attitudes. First, the Eastern countries feel that the deployment of nuclear weapons or their storage inside their territories is (or if it has not taken place, would be) no compensation for the dangers of acquisition of such weapons by the FRG. Since they enjoy the security of the supposed conventional superiority of the Warsaw Pact countries, the capability of the Soviet Union to deliver weapons rapidly to the zone in a crisis and the Soviet IR/MRBM's targeted on the area, they see no need for immediate possession of tactical nuclear weapons. However, one may wonder why, in the face of the assumed tactical nuclear superiority of the NATO countries inside the area, Poland should propose a freeze of this superiority. Perhaps the explanation is that it sees no possibility of inducing the Soviet Union to deploy or store nuclear weapons in peacetime in an area located outside of Soviet territory and even less chance of obtaining such weapons from the Soviet Union for incorporation into its own armaments. If that were the case, a quantitative freeze could not reduce

Poland's chances of attaining a nuclear status, which would be nil anyway, but it would help prevent even greater Western nuclear superiority being established close to her borders. The Poles also regard this as a first step toward complete denuclearization.

Second, the Eastern countries have, or claim to have, a vital interest in preventing West German nuclear armament and, as a consequence, a vital interest in a nuclear transfer freeze.

For the Western countries neither of these reasons for wanting a freeze exists. Most members of NATO, especially the FRG and the United States, consider it vital for purposes of deterrence and defense that tactical nuclear weapons be available to the NATO forces inside the borders of West Germany. They compensate for the inferiority of conventional forces, thereby assuming a major role in deterring or stopping an attack on the FRG. While a freeze would tend to perpetuate the present Western tactical nuclear superiority in Central Europe, there is concern in the West that the existing superiority might not prove sufficient in the future in view of the fact that the Soviet Union would continue to be free to increase the number of its nuclear weapons located in the Western parts of its territory adjoining the denuclearized zone in Central Europe. From the Western standpoint, a freeze might be justified as part of a broader program, which might eventually be worldwide, for preventing production of fissionable materials for weapons purposes.

Moreover, there exists no "Germany in reverse" for the West. None of the Eastern countries in the area has the potentialities attributed to the FRG of becoming an independent nuclear menace. It is improbable that the Eastern countries in the area will procure nuclear weapons for themselves or obtain them from the Soviet Union. If this assumption is correct, the transfer of control of nuclear weapons from the Soviet arsenal to the countries in the area would not constitute a problem for the West. However, there is the possibility of the Soviets arming their own troops in the zone with nuclear weapons (or increasing their deployment as the case might be), which could affect the military *status quo* in favor of the Warsaw Pact countries.

Interest in Supervision. There is a second independent variable: the parties have reason to be more insistent on effective verification the more their opponents intend to evade their obligation. In the case of Poland one should expect particularly strong cumulative effects in the direction of intense supervision arising both from its vital interest in preventing the Germans from obtaining nuclear weapons and from what can be assumed to be its firm conviction that the FRG has strong incentives to seek control over nuclear weapons.

The Eastern parties to a freeze agreement might also suspect the United States of having an incentive to permit German evasions of the agreement. They might reason that if the incentives of the FRG rose very high there would be an intolerable strain on United States-West German relations if the United States insisted on strict compliance with the agreement. They know of the strain on interallied relations that resulted from the attempts of the superpowers to prevent France and Communist China from becoming nuclear powers.

The West, which has been shown to have less interest in the proposed freeze, has also less reason to ascribe to opponents an incentive to evade their obligations under a freeze. The Eastern countries in the area would gain little from supplementing Soviet nuclear armaments and nothing by trying to substitute for the Soviet arsenal a meager nuclear arsenal of their own. Therefore, the West would have less need of verification against evasions of the freeze by the Eastern countries.

The West has slight reason to anticipate a Soviet incentive to circumvent a freeze agreement of the kind suggested by the G Plan. Even when free to act in matters of nuclear deployment, the Soviet Union has abstained from placing nuclear warheads on the territory of its allies.

If only these two determinants of supervision policy needed to be taken into consideration, it would follow that the Eastern parties to a freeze agreement would have reason to be more insistent on effective and intense verification than the West. Yet, this conclusion may be belied by events, because both the East and the West might find it awkward to act accordingly. Having opposed or belittled the value of verification, and having treated it in a cavalier fashion even in the G Plan itself, the Eastern countries could conceivably fear prejudicing their position in other arms control negotiations if they insisted on intense supervision in this instance.

The United States has shown sustained interest in verification. Perhaps it could afford, nevertheless, to promote or accept loose verification of a freeze in Central Europe, because such verification would suffice to protect marginal U.S. interests and would, in fact, serve them by not requiring the FRG to subject itself to intense supervision.

Moreover, in favoring verification as prescribed in the G Plan, the United States would be adhering to its established principle that arms control agreements should not prejudice United States security.

There is no way of predicting whether the third determinant, tradition or inclination, in competition with the two rational determinants, will win out. If it did, the resulting verification policies of the two sides would reflect a peculiarity of the area: strong pressure for intense verification from the Communist countries involved in the negotiations, indifference or even opposition to such verification on the part of the West.

The G Plan, like the R Plan, makes a few broad suggestions concerning the administration of the supervision process and states them in terms of tentative proposals subject to later agreement. However, the G Plan lays down a principle that differs from one contained in the R Plan. The latter calls for a "special control body" to supervise the discharge of the duties proposed. The G Plan calls for the use of "mixed commissions composed of representatives of the Warsaw Pact and of the North Atlantic Treaty Organization on a parity basis" to exercise "supervision and control."

Neither the R Plan nor the G Plan conforms to the suggestions made in Part II of this volume dealing with international organization for the verification of arms control agreements. This case study foresees for the G and R Plans a reciprocal or a mixed system of verification, i.e., a system where reciprocal inspectors are supplemented by international personnel acting as observers. Both a reciprocal and a mixed system avoid the paralysis that may arise from a special control body composed of members from both parties and presumably operating on the principle of unanimity.

A purely reciprocal system, however, might run into serious difficulties if it were made to serve uniformly for the whole freeze area. One can conceive of the FRG and Poland accepting inspectors from each other on their respective territories. But it would take a more radical change in the political climate for a similar exchange of inspectors to be tolerated between the two parts of Germany. The inspectors in that case would all be "Germans," but they might be all the more suspect of conducting activities other than merely supervising the freeze. Most of this trouble could be avoided by selecting mutually acceptable inspectors.

Another way of avoiding difficulties would be to place all supervision in the hands of nationals of the major outside powers, American and Soviet, and perhaps French and British. In the absence of FRG agreement, this would raise the specter of discrimination, the FRG being after all a significant power as well as the chief target of the entire freeze plan and its supervision.

Supervision Applied to the Federal Republic of Germany. Intricate questions are raised by peculiarities in the position of the FRG not only with respect to the merits and demerits of the G Plan itself, but also as regards its supervision.

If it is correct to assume that a primary intent of the G Plan is to prevent West German control of nuclear weapons, the West Germans have reason to suspect that any supervision demanded or accepted by the East is directed primarily at the detection of West German evasion, and allied support of such German evasion. The West Germans will tend to have much greater qualms about intensive verification of the freeze than the other allies in NATO, who would be less affected by inspections at frontier junctions, bases, or plants. They would react sensitively to support or promotion by Western countries of intense verification on West German soil. West Germany as the special target of Eastern suspicions and Communist infiltration, subversion, and expansion, would have reasons for concern, not necessarily shared by her allies, that reciprocal inspection could in her case be abused as a means of military espionage, psychological warfare, and anti-German propaganda. Any alleged German violation of the Plan, for instance, could be turned against the German "fascist, capitalist and militarist enemies of the peace-loving peoples." If West Germany, as a result of denunciations, were subjected to international investigation, new suspicions of her would be aroused even if the denunciations proved unwarranted in the end. While it should be possible to minimize such effects of whatever inspection scheme were chosen, they should not be overlooked. The inevitable strains on Allied relations with the FRG that would arise out of a freeze should not be further exacerbated by supervision procedures. The willingness of the Polish Government to consider other verification proposals than those contained in the G Plan may open the doors for agreements that would not be subject to West German objections.

Verification Organization for the G Plan

The G Plan provides for some commitments which it is not feasible to verify; others would require such a vast organization as to make the verification unfeasible. The organization set forth here is limited to the single function of verifying the commitment that fissionable materials shall not be produced in the area.

The G Plan suggests that "supervision and control" could be exercised by mixed commissions of representatives of the Warsaw Pact and of the North Atlantic Treaty on a parity basis. Those commissions "could be enlarged to include also representatives of other states." The G Plan also envisages periodic meetings of the representatives of the nuclear powers to exchange "all information and reports indispensable for the implementation of the obligations with regard to the freezing of nuclear and thermonuclear armaments."

Inspections of the nature required for a production cutoff could be made by such commissions, although the procedure requires more personnel than a reciprocal inspection. It may be assumed that the members of the inspection team would report their findings to their respective governments. If, for example, the Warsaw Pact representatives disagreed with the findings, the issue would arise in the meetings of the nuclear powers where a split report would probably frustrate any action. However, if the inspection were purely reciprocal, the result would be essentially the same with the split being resolved through normal diplomatic channels rather than through a meeting of the nuclear powers. Therefore, at this stage a split report would have no significance.

Apparently, the G Plan contemplates inspections by commissions of equal numbers of representatives of NATO and Warsaw Pact countries. The meetings, however, would be of representatives of the United States, the United Kingdom, the Soviet Union, and France. In view of past Soviet positions, we may assume that decisions would have to be unanimous. Whether or not such meetings of the nuclear powers would serve a useful purpose would depend largely on the composition of the meetings, the voting procedures, and the possibility of majority decisions for at least some issues.

The G Plan provisions do not rule out inclusion of neutral observers on the inspection teams, and may be sufficiently flexible to permit reciprocal inspection. In the latter event, the required staff could probably be reduced by 25 percent.

At present, the area included in the G Plan contains no facilities where the nuclear product can be transformed into weapons, such as isotope separation plants, chemical processing plants, and fuel fabrication plants utilizing highly enriched uranium. A small chemical processing plant is planned for West Germany to commence operations after 1970.

Czechoslovakia recently announced a power reactor for completion in 1970. Apparently no power reactors are planned for East Germany or Poland. This is logical, since East Germany and Poland produce large quantities of cheap coal, and nuclear power would not be competitive with conventional power for many years. The same situation exists in West Germany. However, the West German nuclear power plants, while they will not produce cheap electricity, are consistent with a long-range planning program for conservation of West German fuel resources. Research reactors exist in all states in the area, but the verification requirements are minimal.

It should be noted that West Germany has agreed with the United States to the institution of safeguards by EURATOM or by the United States to ensure against diversion to weapons purposes of the production of fissionable materials in its planned facilities. EURATOM is required to consult with the IAEA in order to coordinate the safeguards program. The agreements provide for chemical processing of the spent fuel elements either in the United States or in the Eurochemic Plant in Mol, Belgium, which is subject to EURATOM safeguards.

Inspection as envisaged in the G Plan would require approximately eighteen inspectors. Headquarters would have to be established both in West Germany and in one of the Warsaw Pact states to direct the inspection operations, perform and collate the statistical data, and carry out normal administrative functions. The total number of officer personnel in addition to the inspectors required for this purpose might number twenty. Twelve persons should be added for secretarial and other services, making a total staff of fifty. Of this staff, two-thirds should be located in West Germany and one-third in the Warsaw Pact states. The greater number in West Germany reflects the necessity of inspecting declared facilities situated there.

One function of the inspectors in West Germany, and virtually the only function of the inspectors in the Warsaw Pact countries, would be to verify the nonexistence of clandestine facilities for producing fissionable materials. The most suitable procedure for this type of verification would be to permit mobile teams of four or six members to go anywhere in the area. External observation should be sufficient to establish reasonable grounds for believing the existence of major violations. Isotope separation plants and power reactors are reasonably large and have distinct designs. Although chemical processing plants could be located in facilities of conventional design, associated activities such as storage of radioactive fuel elements and waste burial can readily be detected. The inspection teams should have access to data concerning the consumption of electrical power, which is substantial in connection with the most important nuclear facilities.

The system outlined above should give assurance that declared facilities are being utilized solely for non-weapons purposes, and reasonable assurance of the non-existence of clandestine production facilities. This latter conclusion is strengthened by the fact that the easiest method for a nuclear power to violate the commitments of the G Plan would be through transfer of weapons or weapons materials rather than through production in the area.

THE RAPACKI PLAN

The first stage of the R Plan involves the "freezing of nuclear weapons and rockets and prohibition of the establishment of new bases." The Plan prohibits the states within the zone (1) from producing or preparing to produce any kind of nuclear weapons or nuclear delivery vehicles on their territory; (2) from introducing any kind of nuclear weapons or nuclear delivery vehicles; and (3) from granting permission for the establishment of new bases or facilities for the stockpiling or use of nuclear weapons or nuclear delivery vehicles in the zone.

Verification of a commitment not to produce nuclear weapons in the area presents the same considerations as the similar commitment under the G Plan. The nuclear weapons could be produced in the area only from fissionable material produced in, or introduced into, the area. The verification machinery required to prevent production of fissionable material in the area has been outlined above. Verification of the fabrication of weapons from undetected materials in the area would be extremely difficult, if not impossible, and therefore we do not deal with machinery to accomplish this objective.

The commitments not to transfer nuclear delivery vehicles to states within the area, not to introduce new nuclear delivery vehicles, and not to establish new bases or facilities for the stockpiling or use of nuclear weapons or nuclear delivery vehicles require the same type of verification and the same type of organization as one aspect of stage two of the R Plan—the elimination of nuclear delivery vehicles and bases.

Stage two of the R Plan includes two proposals which present separate verification requirements, although they are politically linked. The plan stipulates that the states included in the zone eliminate all nuclear delivery vehicles from their national armaments and reduce military forces to an agreed level with a corresponding reduction of conventional armaments. The states outside the zone are called upon to withdraw from the area of the zone all kinds of nuclear weapons and all facilities for their stockpiling and servicing, as well as all nuclear delivery vehicles permanently or temporarily stationed in the zone and all facilities for their servicing, and to reduce their military forces stationed in the area of the zone to an agreed level with a corresponding reduction of their armaments.

The two proposals, elimination of nuclear armaments and reduction of conventional armaments, are part of a single package in that the reduction of conventional armaments is apparently intended to compensate the West for the disadvantages it would expect to suffer from the denuclearization of the area. The two proposals will be treated separately in the discussion that follows.

Elimination of Nuclear Armaments and Their Delivery Systems

The R Plan defines the term "elimination" and distinguishes between elimination in the case of states inside and states outside the area. States in the area are called upon to eliminate nuclear delivery vehicles, presumably on the assumption that these states possess no warheads or facilities to stockpile them. The outside powers are required to

54

withdraw from the area all kinds of nuclear weapons and all facilities for their stockpiling and servicing, and to withdraw all nuclear delivery vehicles and all facilities for their servicing.

To achieve its end, such a plan must include two processes: first, withdrawing all the elements that exist in the area at the time the agreement goes into effect (denuclearization) and second, the non-reintroduction of any nuclear elements into the area during the duration of the agreement (non-renuclearization).

The verification of non-renuclearization has been treated implicity in the discussion of the proposal for a quantitative nuclear freeze under the G Plan, since production of new nuclear armaments in the area or introduction from the outside are the only two means by which renuclearization could take place. The transfer freeze, which figures prominently in the G Plan and stage one of the R Plan, does not present a separate problem either in the case of denuclearization or of renuclearization because the withdrawal of nuclear elements would be required as well as the prevention of subsequent re-introduction into the area no matter under whose control the nuclear elements would be.

The task of verifying denuclearization—the elimination of all existing elements of nuclear power in the area—is quite distinct from anything connected with a mere freeze. The freeze deals exclusively with future actions by the parties to the agreement, whereas denuclearization is directed at undoing what one or more of the parties have undertaken previously. Since the states of the area have no nuclear weapons nor significant quantities of fissionable materials at their disposal, denuclearization can only apply to the weapons of the major nuclear powers in the area.

There are two ways in which verification of denuclearization can be accomplished, by verifying that all the elements of nuclear power known to exist in the area are being physically removed from the area, or by verifying that, irrespective of what elements may have existed there previously, the area itself has been cleared of all such elements by the denuclearization process. Both methods offer advantages and, at the same time, pose difficulties.

Under the first method, withdrawal from the area is much easier to verify than introduction into the area. In the case of a freeze or of non-renuclearization, the inspected country has an interest, if it wants to violate the agreement, in producing secretly or in smuggling into the area the forbidden elements. In the case of a commitment to withdraw nuclear elements that are known to the adversary, the inspected country has an interest not only to disclose all of its withdrawals but, if possible, to make them appear more comprehensive than they really are, e.g., by exporting dummies while retaining the actual elements. This, however, could presumably be detected. The difficulty lies in verifying that all the existing elements have been eliminated. This can be accomplished only if prior to the process of withdrawal a complete and reliable inventory could be compiled of all nuclear elements existing in the area.

Such stocktaking presents no insuperable obstacle to verification in the case of bulky and easily detectable elements such as bases or large bombers and rockets. Here, national intelligence may have established and kept up a reliable inventory, or be able to do so by means of aerial or space photography. But in calling for the controlled elimination of all nuclear elements, including all rockets, small as well as large, and of all nuclear warheads, the plan sets a task that does not appear to be fully realizable.[2] However, it should be noted that a less than foolproof system of verification would not necessarily affect U.S. interests adversely. On the contrary, an all-pervasive, presumably adversary search for hidden elements in the possession of nuclear forces would probably make it difficult, if not impossible, for the United States to maintain forces in the area. West Germany, too, would be likely to balk at inspection that would make it the duty of foreign inspectors to look into practically everything that could serve as a cover or container of hidden nuclear elements.[3]

Under the second method, no inventory of existing elements is required. But the verification of a negative fact, in this case that after the parties allege to have fulfilled their obligations no nuclear elements remain in the area, is an even more exacting task. The inspectors would have only national intelligence to tell them what existed before and has allegedly been withdrawn (or destroyed), and they would have to search everywhere for elements that allegedly do not exist. The question is how intense and reliable the verification of denuclearization and non-renuclearization would have to be to satisfy the parties.

In contrast to what was found to be the case if a mere freeze were to be verified, the West has a great interest that verification of the elimination of the main elements of nuclear power from the area be highly reliable. American military power in the area is the chief target because the United States relies heavily on tactical nuclear weapons deployed inside the area and would stand to lose seriously if, after eliminating its nuclear weapons and delivery vehicles from the area, the other side were found to possess substantial tactical nuclear firepower. For the countries in the Eastern part, much less would be at stake in case of a violation of the agreement by the West because the Eastern countries would be better off than in the face of the present Western nuclear superiority which at least would have been whittled down.

Thus, whichever of the two methods of verification is used, they would have to promise a high degree of effectiveness.

The Reduction of Armed Forces and Conventional Armaments

Under the R Plan, there would be two agreed levels of forces and armaments: one for those states within the zone and one for the forces in the zone from states outside the zone. The levels are not specified in the R Plan.

The objects of verification might fall into, but not necessarily be limited to, the following categories: aircraft; bases (active and inactive); and strength and deployment of active forces, including active reserves. Furthermore, an agreed limitation should require that the limitations would not be offset by augmentations such as excessive personnel recruiting and mobilization and undue manufacture and acquisition of armaments. In any case, the objects of verification must be important and easy to detect and to identify if a high degree of confidence is to be expected.

Organization for Stages I and II of the Rapacki Plan

The R Plan calls for a "system of strict international control and inspection on the ground and in the air." The G Proposals call for a "system of supervision and safeguards," but both say little about administrative organization. The two Plans differ with respect to the administration of supervision. The R Plan suggests the establishment of a "special control body" open to later agreement. The G Plan proposes commissions composed of representatives of the Warsaw Pact and North Atlantic Treaty on a parity basis and periodic meetings of states whose armed forces are stationed in the area.

It is probable that neither the idea of a control body nor that of a parity commission would prove an acceptable substitute for the reciprocal or the mixed system discussed previously in connection with the G Plan. A "body" would raise voting questions of enormous difficulty, whereas commissions based on parity would foreshadow paralysis rather than effectiveness of the system. A verification system based on the reciprocal concept would probably be more suitable. Several organizational alternatives are available within the reciprocal concept: (1) organizations composed of the states within the zone (West Germany, East Germany, Poland, and Czechoslovakia); (2) reciprocal organizations composed of the NATO and Warsaw Pact countries; (3) reciprocal organizations composed of states outside the zone with forces in the zone (the United States, the United Kingdom, and France verifying East Germany, Poland, and Czechoslovakia; the Soviet Union verifying West Germany); and (4) a mixed system organized along the lines of alternative three above with the inclusion of international observers.

Owing to the political situation existing between East and West Germany, we have excluded the first alternative from our considerations.

Under the second alternative—reciprocal organizations composed of NATO and Warsaw Pact countries respectively—relations between the FRG and Poland could make the reciprocal deployment of inspectors from these two countries a delicate matter and could seriously affect the operation. At this time, it seems preferable that the verification organization under the West be composed of the United States, the United Kingdom, and France, and the organization under the East of the Soviet Union (alternative 3): factors influencing this preference are that these larger countries have greater resources and are better able to bear the costs.

A mixed system which would include international observers could also be employed. The international observers would provide greater credence for the findings of the reciprocal inspectors. If a mixed system were deemed necessary, the observers might be chosen from neutral states.

Under the reciprocal organization composed of the United States, the United Kingdom, and France, affiliation with NATO's extensive radar warning system, an excellent network of communications, and the availability of personnel and material resources would significantly increase the effectiveness of the verification process. A coordinated arrangement could be worked out in a committee made up of the United States, the United Kingdom, and France to provide general and specific direction to the Administrator of the Allied Verification Organization.[4] The committee would cooperate with NATO components for mutual support, common and combined usage of facilities, resources and training programs, and the elimination of duplication.

Western Verification Organization. The organization would have an Administrator, a Headquarters Unit, and Control Units as follows: two in East Germany, four in Poland, and three in Czechoslovakia (see Table 2–1). It would be integrated to allow the Administrator to exercise maximum control over the organization and elements attached to it. He would operate under the direction of the higher organization. Command and control of the Western Verification Organization units in the host countries would not be under the personnel of the host country. There would be occasions when liaison personnel from the host country might be of service to a Western unit in a host country. Liaison personnel, however, should not constitute an element vested with authority to restrict or veto the actions of a Western verification unit in carrying out its duties. Of course, verification personnel would be required to abide by the ground rules agreed upon by states-parties to the agreement.

Control Units in the three states would report directly to the Administrator at the Headquarters of the Western Verification Organization.

Table 2–1. Western Verification Organization Personnel Recapitulation

	Hqtrs. Unit	Control Units								
		1	2	3	4	5	6	7	8	9
Administrator	1									
Supervisor		1	1	1	1	1	1	1	1	1
Assistant	18	1	1	1	1	1	1	1	1	1
Legal	1									
Clerical	8	2	2	2	2	2	2	2	2	2
Communications	16	4	4	4	4	4	4	4	4	4
Transportation										
Aviation	11	6	6	6	6	6	6	6	6	6
Motor	13	2	2	2	2	2	2	2	2	2
Supply	2									
Purchasing	1									
Finance	1									
Interpreters	3	1	1	1	1	1	1	1	1	1
Security	8	5	5	5	5	5	5	5	5	5
Medical	2	1	1	1	1	1	1	1	1	1
Inspectors										
Mobile		24	24	24	24	24	24	24	24	24
Observation Posts[1]		36	27	54	72	18	72	36	27	36
Sub-Total	85	83	74	101	119	65	119	83	74	83
20% Non-Available Factor[2]	17	17	15	20	23	13	23	17	15	17
Total	102	100	89	121	142	78	142	100	89	100
Grand Total	1063									

[1] Number of Posts × 9 observers. Post per control unit: Unit #1—4 posts; #2—3; #3—6; #4—8; #5—2; #6—8; #7—4; #8—3; #9—4.
[2] Flexible allowance for leaves, illness, etc.

The Administrator would report to the next higher organization as established by the signatories.

If international observers augment the verification organization, their reports should be sent to their sponsor and the Administrator of the Western Verification Organization. The primary functions of the formal overt verification organization would be restricted to data collection and reporting. Functions such as the evaluation of data reported, the determination of the existence of substantive or procedural violations, and decisions as to response would rest with the signatory governments.

In addition to the interplay of other verification techniques, many of which are organically external to the verification organization, the organic inspection techniques employed by the Western Verification Organization in the territories being inspected would primarily consist of

TABLE 2–2. Eastern Verification Organization Personnel Recapitulation

	Hqtrs. Unit	Control Units			
		A	B	C	D
Administrator	1				
Supervisors		1	1	1	1
Assistants	12	1	1	1	1
Legal	1				
Clerical	8	2	2	2	2
Communications	16	4	4	4	4
Transportation					
Aviation	7	6	6	6	6
Motor	13	2	2	2	2
Supply	2				
Purchasing	1				
Finance	1				
Interpreters	1	1	1	1	1
Security	8	5	5	5	5
Medical	2	1	1	1	1
Inspectors					
Mobile		24	24	24	24
Observation Posts[1]		72	27	18	36
Sub-Total	73	119	74	65	83
20% Non-Available Factor[2]	15	23	15	13	17
Total	88	142	89	78	100
Grand Total	497				

[1] Number of posts × 9 observers. Post per control unit: Unit A—8; B—3; C—2; D—4.

[2] Flexible allowance for leaves, illness, etc.

mobile teams and observation posts. Mobile teams under a control unit head would operate over large areas and carry out their verification functions by visits at many points. Observation posts under a control unit head would operate with some degree of mobility on a twenty-four hour basis at fixed areas. Surveillance of relevant traffic would be their primary function.

Eastern Verification Organization. Based on the assumptions and criteria related to the Western Verification Organization,[5] the hypothetical counterpart Eastern Verification Organization could be structured with an Administrator, a Headquarters Unit, and four Control Units in West Germany (see Table 2–2).

CONCLUSION

This study has considered the deployment of a Western Verification Organization in the host countries of East Germany, Poland and Czechoslovakia plus a Headquarters Unit possibly in West Berlin and an Eastern Verification Organization in West Germany. Our hypothetical Western Organization has a total of 1063 persons, with 497 for the Eastern Organization.

The most important methods of verification are resident ground verification of declared facilities and installations and mobile ground verification to detect clandestine operations. These methods of verification could be supplemented by exchange of military missions, governmental budget and economic record verification, and verification by aircraft and satellites.

The suggested verification organization is suitable, with varying degrees of assurance, for determining that declared nuclear facilities are being used solely for non-weapons purposes, for the detection of a freeze of large nuclear delivery vehicles, the elimination of large nuclear delivery vehicles, the elimination of large conventional armaments, and clandestine production of fissionable materials. But the suggested verification organization, by itself, could not give adequate assurance of non-fulfillment of commitments concerning troop reductions or ceilings, clandestine manufacture of small armaments, clandestine arms traffic in an area not under surveillance from an observation post, undeclared hidden stockpiles of nuclear weapons, and vehicles suitable for delivery of both nuclear and conventional warheads.

The capabilities and reliability of verification techniques are influenced by the freedom of movement and access that are permitted by a country being verified. Freedom of movement and access must be adequate for the accomplishment of the mission, and anything short of adequate should not be dependent upon or tolerated in an agreement or in actual verification operations. Access and true freedom of movement require organization flexibility, instant communications, command and control, and administrative support.

THE U.S. PROPOSAL FOR A FREEZE OF STRATEGIC NUCLEAR DELIVERY VEHICLES

On January 21, 1964, the President of the United States, in a message to the ENDC at Geneva, submitted several proposals for collateral measures that could be implemented prior to agreement on GCD. The second proposal, a verified freeze of the number and characteristics of strategic nuclear offensive and defensive vehicles, is evaluated in this study in the context of requisite international arrangements to ensure effective verification.[1] It should be noted that this study is limited to the 1964 American proposal for a freeze of strategic delivery systems in which the primary verification technique would be confined to visual observation of gross external characteristics. It does not discuss possible modifications in this type of proposal nor variations in the verification techniques.

In this proposal the numbers and characteristics of strategic nuclear delivery vehicles are divided into five categories: (1) ground-based surface-to-surface missiles having a range of 5,000 kilometers or greater and their associated launching facilities, and sea-based surface-to-surface missiles having a range of 100 kilometers or greater and their associated launchers; (2) strategic bombers having an empty weight of 40,000 kilograms or greater and any associated air-to-surface missiles having a range of 100 kilometers or greater; (3) ground-based surface-to-surface missiles having a range of between 1,000 and 5,000 kilometers and their associated launching facilities; (4) strategic bombers having an empty weight of being between 25,000 and 40,000 kilograms and any associated air-to-surface missiles having a range of 100 kilometers or greater; and (5) strategic anti-missile systems and their associated launching facilities.

These five categories are subject to minimal definitional confusion and, in the current U.S.-Soviet context, are clearly strategic in nature. Nonetheless, there are marginal areas. A nuclear weapon, for example, can be fired by some artillery pieces which fire conventional warheads. So-called tactical missiles and aircraft may also be used strategically to attack large concentrations of population or other strategic targets.

The purpose of the freeze proposal is to prohibit the production of new types of armaments that fall within the aforementioned five categories and to halt the production of all existing types of armaments within these categories and of specified major sub-assemblies of these armaments. Certain narrow exceptions would be permitted; i.e., production to cover the maintenance of vehicles, their accidental loss, and the expenditure of missiles within agreed annual quotas for confidence and training firings. In consonance with production restrictions, the construction and improvement of launching facilities would also be regulated. Testing would be restricted to firings for confidence and training purposes.

Missile replacement would be on a one-for-one basis of the same type of vehicle and based on agreed annual numbers amounting to a small percentage of the inventories of armaments possessed by the respective parties at the effective date of the freeze agreement. The agreed replacement quota would be subject to periodic review, although it is noteworthy that verification of the inventories of armaments possessed by the respective parties would not be required. There is ambiguity with respect to replacing armaments no longer in production. The United States proposal provides that the parties would seek to agree upon acceptable substitutes from among weapons in production, but it is contemplated that a party could reopen production on a one-for-one basis in the event no agreement is reached on the substitute items in production. It is not clear whether a formal refusal for substitution would have to be obtained before the second alternative would be available.

The freeze proposal contains several provisions affecting areas related to but not directly within the five categories of stragetic nuclear delivery vehicles. The potential conversion of transport or other aircraft and of space boosters into delivery vehicles capable of carrying nuclear weapons would be guarded against by a provision authorizing occasional unannounced inspections of facilities no longer (but still capable of) producing specified armaments and by a provision allowing the production of aircraft and space boosters to be monitored.

The freeze proposal would also require that appropriate notice of the planned production of space boosters and advance notice of the time and launch-site location of all space launchings be given by the parties. The purpose of the production notice would be to afford reasonable assurance against stockpiling; the nature of the payload would not have to be disclosed. With respect to advance notice of launchings, notification would be given in sufficient time to permit on-site observation of vehicles prior to launch.

The importance of the space launching provisions is readily apparent when one considers that by 1967 the United States and the Soviet Union had orbited more than 400 space vehicles. Space programs of this magnitude offer ample opportunity to test and develop boosters which can have roles in missile programs as well as in space. Without an appropriate system of verification it would be possible to produce space boosters in such quantities as would affect the replacement scheme for keeping the number of missiles at agreed levels, and it would be possible to make improvements in the characteristics of missiles by actually testing newly developed components and sub-systems under the guise of space launchings. It also would be possible to conduct research and development tests and evaluations of missiles with slight chance of detection by tying the experiments to space packages.

The proposed freeze is concerned not only with the numbers of strategic delivery vehicles but also with their characteristics. In order to prevent a "quality race," in which improved offensive or defensive systems are achieved by redesigning existing systems to make up in quality what they lack in quantity, the United States freeze proposal provides for the monitoring of research and development at the testing stage. For example, compliance with a test ban on nuclear strategic delivery vehicles would be verified by radar monitoring, by inspection of test sites, and by other methods. Moreover, prohibiting tests of new strategic nuclear delivery vehicles would diminish the destabilizing effect of military research and development because a state's military forces are normally reluctant to rely upon an untested weapon for security.

The potentially disruptive effects of technological developments upon national security would give rise to difficulty in planning an effective verification organization for this area of concern. It is likely that, initially at least, a verification organization would have a small role in this area and that parties would rely upon their own sources of information concerning new technological developments.

VERIFICATION OF THE PROPOSED NUCLEAR FREEZE

After the freeze agreement is concluded, but prior to its implementation, the contracting parties would make a complete declaration of all production facilities covered by the agreement and of armament production quotas required by the agreement.[2] The declaration would be kept current as additional facilities capable of producing or assembling the specified armaments and sub-assemblies were converted or constructed. These latter facilities would be declared upon the commencement of conversion or construction.

This section considers the objectives and techniques of the several types of verification contemplated in the U.S. freeze proposal. An attempt is made to estimate the requirements of personnel and equipment needed to carry out such verification. Problems presented by particular types of verification in relation to the level of performance expected from them are also examined.

Declared Facilities No Longer Producing the Affected Armaments and Specified Sub-Assemblies

According to the U.S. concept of an initial check, inspectors would examine declared facilities to ensure that they have been dismantled, closed, or converted to other production activities. The initial inspection would include an examination of all manufacturing areas of a facility, a task that ordinarily could be accomplished in the course of several days. It is also contemplated that occasional unannounced checks of these facilities after the initial inspection would be adequate, because the freeze proposal assumes that many months are required to set up the production lines of the specified armaments and sub-assemblies and to attain a reasonable production rate.

The verification procedures for declared facilities which have been completely dismantled or closed would be relatively simple. However, those declared facilities converted to other production activities would present a problem, if the converted plant were producing or manufacturing products which were similar to some degree to those parts used in the affected armaments and major sub-assemblies. The U.S. proposal does not include verification provisions as elaborate as those suggested in some studies.[3] In the case of declared operating production facilities and converted activities, inspectors would verify only agreed numbers and configurations of specified items being produced for the purpose of replacement or allowed missile firings. Whereas numbers would be of crucial importance in declared operating facilities, a visual inspection in a converted plant might not be sufficient to alert an inspector to the manufacturing of items usable in specified armaments and major sub-assemblies. Nonetheless, visual observation of external characteristics might be useful and the verification organization postulated in this study provides for this function.

One study has concluded that the following sub-assemblies and major components of strategic nuclear delivery vehicles could be detected by visual observation:[4]

I. Sub-assemblies
    A. Re-entry vehicles
    B. Inter-stage structures
    C. Liquid fuel tanks
    D. Solid propellant motors
    E. Aft skirt

II. Major Components
    A. Liquid engine
        1. Thrust chamber
        2. Injector dome
    B. Solid motor
        1. Casing
        2. Aft closure
        3. Graphite ring
        4. Nozzles
    C. Re-entry vehicles
        1. Forging
        2. Heat shields

III. Aircraft
    Fuselage
        1. Bomb-bay structure
        2. Radar Radome
        3. Bomb sight

IV. Ship Hulls
    Although existing hulls or existing-type hulls might be used, deviations from the conventional ship design might include missile handling and storage equipment and facilities, missile guidance components, and increased security surrounding the construction and fitting out of the ships.

V. Mobile Launchers
    Mobile launchers are generally designed as single purpose vehicles, and for missiles of the ranges involved in the freeze proposal, the missile-handling gear would be distinctive although the engine, chassis, and tracks might be multipurpose standard equipment.

Observation of any of the above components and sub-assemblies in a declared facility alleged to be converted to other production activities would indicate the freeze agreement is being violated.

A trained two-man team would probably suffice to conduct the initial check of a declared facility. No unique equipment would be necessary. Qualified personnel may be drawn from the United States and the Soviet Union, as well as a number of other states engaged in missile and rocket programs.

Monitoring Allowed Production of Specified Armaments and Major Sub-Assemblies

The object of this verification provision is to ensure that the annual quota of the specified armaments and major sub-assemblies would not be exceeded. The U.S. freeze proposal requires the parties to agree upon: (1) lists of armaments affected by the agreements; (2) lists of non-strategic and non-military vehicles possessing weight, thrust, and range characteristics falling within the categories of the agreement; (3) lists of specific major sub-assemblies affected by the agreement; (4) lists indicating which of a party's armaments are considered to be of the same type and describing each model within a type by gross external characteristics, such as major dimensions and gross configuration; (5) annual production quotas for each of the specified armaments and sub-assembly replacements; and (6) arrangements relating to verification, such as the annual quota of inspections and the rights of inspectors.[5] With regard to major sub-assemblies under point (3), the United States believes that the following should be included: (a) for ballistic missiles—liquid rocket engines and tankage, solid rocket motors, stage assemblies, and motor launchers; and (b) for cruise-type missiles and aircraft—fuselages.[6]

Monitoring the production of the specified armaments and major sub-assemblies in a declared facility with resident inspectors is a straightforward procedure. Exact production figures on these items is neither feasible nor absolutely necessary. Inspection should produce a reasonably accurate estimate that can be relied upon with confidence. The verification personnel must be furnished with accurate data and descriptions of the items to be verified and must have at their disposal reliable means for communicating their findings to higher echelons. In the absence of special sensors, it is probable that each facility encompassed by the verification would require one or two inspectors per shift.

Observation of Vehicle Attrition by Destruction

From time to time vehicles and their components would have to be removed from the inventory for reasons such as chemical deterioration, corrosion, or structural fatigue. Such removal and replacement may occur at the expiry of the "shelf-life" of particular components or may be the result of equipment failures experienced in periodic tests of the various systems and sub-systems of the delivery vehicles. The purpose of verification in this area would be to guarantee that the items declared for destruction are, in fact, destroyed and that the "replacement guarantee" did not become a technique for altering the original item so as to upgrade its characteristics.

Verification of destruction would be simply a matter of observing that the object in question was physically altered to the point of being rendered useless. Protection against retro-fitting and up-grading the destroyed object would be provided by verification at the production and testing phase. Several appropriately trained two-man inspection teams should suffice to verify the destruction process. No unique equipment should be necessary.

Observation of Space Launchings and Missile Firings

The ostensible purpose of verifying space launchings and missile firings is to determine whether the vehicles produced have in reality been consumed. More important is to prevent clandestine research and development testing. The United States freeze proposal does not expressly restrict the number and nature of space launchings, but there are limitations on the types of authorized missile firings. Such firings may be conducted only for confidence and training tests, not for research and development of new missiles or modifications of existing missiles. Without detailed information on the rocket engines, airframes, guidance systems, and propellants, and without technical monitoring of the parameters measured on board the vehicle, and as reported to the party conducting the launching or firing, a highly-skilled, well-trained, and optimally located observer could verify merely that the gross configuration and characteristics of the vehicle whose firing he observed were generally those of other vehicles in the same category.[7]

With regard to missiles fired from submarines or ships, the U.S. proposal calls for sufficient advance notice to permit observation vessels to be in the vicinity. There is no requirement of pre-launch inspection in such circumstances, and only a minimum number of personnel would be necessary for what essentially is an accounting operation. Observations of missile and space-vehicle launchings on land would be conducted at the launching site from the time of final check-out of the vehicle through the countdown and launching. At least one observer should be stationed in the blockhouse to view the vehicle through periscopes and closed circuit television monitoring systems in order to ensure that nothing was added to the vehicle during the final moments of preparation for launching. The observer also could watch for color changes, etc., suggestive of the testing of different fuel and oxidizer combinations in the propellant system.

Small teams of five to seven verifying personnel would probably be sufficient to observe launchings. By working in shifts from the time notification of an impending launch was received until the vehicle was launched, the observers should be able to detect any attempted substitution or alterations that would be noticeable through visual observation of gross characteristics. At unusually active launch complexes it might be desirable to station several teams on site in order to view operations simultaneously.

Being limited to physical observation of gross characteristics, the observers would need little in the way of equipment. Photography might be useful, as would ready-identification aids. The observers also should be made aware of other data, including the number of stages, configuration of payload, external dimensions, type of propellant, and number of vernier engines.

Confirmation of Vehicle Attrition by Accidental Losses

The purpose of such confirmation is to verify statements that vehicles have in fact been lost through accidental means. This is necessary to ensure that vehicles produced as replacements for accidentally lost vehicles are actually replacements and are not being used for augmentation purposes. Accidental loss assumes that there can be no advance notice or pre-destruction inspection.

The possibility of a violation in the event of vehicle attrition losses depends upon two factors: (1) the type of vehicle; (2) the area in which the loss allegedly occurred. There is little likelihood of violation when an accidental loss involves a readily identifiable vehicle in a relatively accessible region. Difficulties increase when the debris has been damaged to such an extent that there is some question as to precisely what the item had been before it was destroyed. An even greater problem arises when the debris cannot be located or a vehicle is lost in an inaccessible area.

In such situations, confirmation by means other than on-site physical inspection would have to be worked out.

Verification under this scheme appears to require little elaboration of physical on-site inspection previously discussed. The state reporting the loss would merely declare the type of vehicle involved and the area in which the loss took place. Following this declaration, the inspecting party would go to the site of the loss and make its verification. In cases where physical inspection was impossible, it might be necessary to turn to secondary evidence such as flight recordings, telemetery records, or films. The inspecting country might also have unilateral means of verifying certain of these accidents.

It would probably be possible, given the similarities in training, to use the same inspection teams available for verification of attrition by destruction. Normally, special equipment would not be needed for verification of accidental losses, but attention should be given to state-of-the-art improvements in undersea observation that could assure confirmation of the loss of missile-laden submarines in deep water.

If the freeze were effective, the number of vehicles in inventory should not increase and the risk of accident should be affected accordingly, especially since military research and development testing of strategic nuclear delivery vehicles, which are important causes of accidents, would be prohibited.

Inspection Relating to Limitations on Launchers

The freeze proposal would require the parties to declare for each type of launcher and launching facility[8] discussed below: the facilities producing mobile launchers; the annual production quota to be produced; all installations to be used for space vehicle launching and all sites to be used for firings of vehicles affected by the agreement; notice of the nature of any mobile or stationary launchers to be destroyed because of natural attrition. Accidental losses or destruction of launchers normally would be verified by on-site inspection. If this were not feasible, confirmation of such loss or destruction would be necessary, assuming in each case that a replacement allowance was being sought.

Launching facilities for ground-based surface-to-surface missiles having a range of 5,000 kilometers or greater. Visual external observation could detect replacement or construction operations at the launching sites, although the inspectors might not readily notice hidden improvements that could be installed in launchers. Close familiarity with the construction and improvement specifications and attentive observation of any work performed according to the specifications would be required on the part of the inspectors.

Launchers for seabased surface-to-air missiles having a range of 100 kilometers or greater. These launchers may be of an underwater or a surface type. Launchers which consist of tubes built into the hull of a submarine would be difficult to conceal during the hull construction phase and even after the submarine is built, if factors susceptible to external detection are evident. The same would be true of launchers for surface firings of missiles on submarines and surface ships. Such launchers would be detectable by human visual observation of the gross external characteristics.

70

Launching facilities for ground-based surface-to-surface missiles having a range of 1,000 to 5,000 kilometers. These launchers fall into two categories; those requiring stationary facilities and those which are mobile. The verification-confidence factor of stationary launchers would be comparable to the launchers associated with missiles with a range of 5,000 kilometers or greater. The situation is different in the case of mobile launchers. Under the U.S. proposal, the parties would declare the facilities producing mobile launchers, decide on the annual production quotas of the mobile launchers to be produced, and determine the specific launchers affected by the agreement.

With the above information on facilities, production quotas, and affected launchers, plus a knowledge of gross characteristics of the launchers involved, verification would present no great problem. Since some improvements might not be detected by visual observation, the verification-confidence factor would increase only as more detailed inspections were permitted. Mobile launchers which were not declared could easily escape detection particularly if they were improvised rigs or were capable of being assembled or disassembled at any location.

One or two resident inspectors per shift ordinarily should be sufficient at each facility producing, replacing, constructing, or improving launchers. Extra staff would not be needed for visual verification of the production of mobile and sea-borne launchers at declared facilities producing other specified armaments and major sub-assemblies.

Verification of Undeclared Facilities

Verification of undeclared facilities differs from inspection of declared facilities primarily in that in the former case there would be no formal announcement to initiate the verification process. The system would require some other impetus to get it under way, such as information from verification teams engaged in the inspection of declared facilities or from national intelligence systems. The first type might consist of leads derived from shipping activities or from conversations regarding the whereabouts of personnel in pertinent related activities or other by-products of observation. The latter might be based on any kind of intelligence gathering or analysis.

Presumably such data would be studied by the receiving state in the same manner as other information important to national security. If, at the governmental level, it should be determined that an inspection was necessary, the teams without being informed why an inspection was being made would perform their tasks and submit their reports just as in the case of declared facilities or activities.

ORGANIZATIONS FOR VERIFICATION

There are several ways in which a body entrusted with verification of a nuclear freeze might be organized. This section evaluates the features of reciprocal and mixed systems of inspection.

Whatever type of verification organization is created its inspectors must possess a rapid, reliable, and secure communications network for the transmission of data to an evaluation center. Second, greater economy in personnel, materiel, and money might be realized if the logistical and administrative support units were unified to the maximum degree consistent with effective data-collection. Where consistent with efficiency and security, it might be desirable to permit the host country to supply housing, food, fuel, and unsensitive administrative and maintenance services. Some flexibility would be afforded the inspecting organization if it were to be permitted to operate and maintain its own transportation. Third, an adequate budget must be assured to the organization. Under a pure reciprocal system, each state would finance its own inspection operations, and the same procedure could be followed under a mixed system. Under an international organizational arrangement incorporating a mixed system, the former could serve as a clearing house for financial matters by billing the inspecting state for expenses incidental to its verification operations, thereby ameliorating the task of negotiating an agreement to govern an international budget. Fourth, the movement and access rights of verification personnel should be clearly defined in advance and scrupulously adhered to.

Reciprocal Systems

Under the United States proposal, verification would be reciprocal; that is, would be carried out by a party other than the state whose territory or facility is being inspected.[9] Many of the specific items mentioned previously lend themselves most readily to reciprocal verification. This would be true of verification of vehicle attrition by destruction and of verification of announced missile and space vehicle launchings. Ordinarily, a mixed or international verification team would not be needed since the nature of the task amounts to merely observing and certifying to the reciprocal state that certain declared objects were destroyed or used.

The verification of accidental losses by on-site inspection could also be accomplished under the reciprocal system. There might be merit, however, to having other states participate in an inspection when there was doubt as to what was accidentally lost or destroyed in order to support a demand for more definite proof of the loss if replacement were sought.

The reciprocal system would be satisfactory for conducting initial checks of declared facilities no longer producing specified armaments and sub-assemblies and for verifying that annual production quotas of replacement armaments and specified major sub-assemblies were not being exceeded.

The reciprocal system would be preferable for verifying that no undeclared production facilities were in operation and that unauthorized launcher construction and improvement activities were not occurring. Completely national inspection units could better protect the secrecy of an impending surprise inspection, and potential disclosures of matters involving the national security of the inspected state would receive less publicity. Nevertheless, there would be an advantage to having foreign observers present when violations were detected or when it was necessary to prove such violations.

The pure reciprocal system would be workable so long as not more than four or five states actively participated in the freeze. As the number of states increased, the number of inspecting teams simultaneously visiting an individual facility, particularly when a destruction event or missile firing has been scheduled would become unmanageable. When this point was reached, there would be several alternatives worth exploring.

The first alternative would entail the formation of consolidated inspection teams to which each state might contribute a representative. Thus, only one team would conduct a given inspection, but it would be composed of representatives of all the other states involved. Although the number of independent teams in a state at any given time would diminish under this scheme, formidable language, logistic, and administrative problems would have to be resolved.

The second alternative within the reciprocal concept involves a "pooling" of functions. The states concerned would reach agreements as to who would inspect what. The data would be available to all participants, but certain states would tend to become specialists in a particular type of inspection. Although this scheme also would reduce the number of independent teams in the field, it probably would require too much in the way of advance negotiation and agreement to be feasible at the onset of the freeze. On the other hand, it would have merit as an experiment in developing specializations for later use in an international verification organization.

The third alternative is based on a "pairing-off" among geographically proximate states. Certain states would become responsible for inspecting certain territories or nations, the data being available to all participants. However, given the high degree of trust needed among the states, the idea would not be practicable at the beginning of the freeze.

Mixed Systems

The mixed system discussed below fuses the reciprocal and international elements. The idea underlying the "mix" is to obtain more credibility for the verification system by adding an impartial international element: allegations of violation would be predicated on data supplied by both international and national members of a team. Moreover, the mixed system would provide training and experience required to staff a future, more comprehensive international organization, would help to bring world opinion to bear on violations, and would enlarge participation to include more than just the major military powers.

At present, there is no international organization designated for the freeze proposal. Conceivably, the international element of a mixed system for verification might derive from LIDO designed to verify several partial measures in the arms control field (discussed in Part II of this volume). In the event an international disarmament organization for Stage I of a GCD were established, the responsibilities of the limited organization could be taken over. In any case, an international body involved in a mixed system should be structured to provide international observers as requested by reciprocal parties, receive reports from both the international observers and reciprocal parties, publish and keep records of such reports, provide its own internal administrative and logistical support, and defray its expenses by apportioning them among its members.

Under the mixed system, the plan of operation would be based upon coordination rather than integration. Reciprocal inspectors and international observers would at all times be responsible to their respective sponsors and remain subject to their administrative and operational control. The senior reciprocal inspector of the mixed team would act as coordinator and have the authority to seek consultation on the part of the international element for the purpose of setting forth the objectives, methods, and procedures to be followed. However, authority exercised by the reciprocal unit of the mixed system would not extend to the administration, discipline, internal organization, or training of the international component, unless the latter so requested.

Because of the number of variables and unknown factors, it is impracticable to construct an organization in detail for the fulfillment of tasks emanating from a nuclear freeze treaty. Nevertheless, some approximation of the scale of organization involved in administering and verifying the freeze outlined in the United States proposal can be worked out. These are presented in tabular form in the accompanying tables under mixed organizational schemes. The personnel requirements of a pure reciprocal system may be determined by eliminating the international element in parentheses in the first and fourth arrangements of Tables 3–1 and 3–2.

The numbers of inspectors required to perform verification tasks of a freeze are estimated as follows:

1. *Monitoring Allowed Production at Declared Facilities*
   (*including initial checks*)

Reciprocal System	2	inspectors per shift
Mixed System	2	reciprocal inspectors and
	1	international observer per shift

2. *Inspecting Undeclared Facilities*
   Teams of varying size drawn from pool

3. *Observing Space Launchings and Missile Firings*

Reciprocal System	5-7	inspectors from pool per team
Mixed System	1	international observer from pool per reciprocal team

4. *Verifying Destruction and Accidental Loss of Strategic Nuclear Delivery Vehicles and Launchers*

Reciprocal System	2	inspectors from pool per team
Mixed System	2	reciprocal inspectors and
	1	international observer drawn from pool

5. *Checking Declared Facilities No Longer Producing Affected Items*

Reciprocal System	2	inspectors from pool
Mixed System	2	reciprocal inspectors and
	1	international observer drawn from pools

6. *Other Related Tasks*
   Teams drawn from pools

Table 3–1 illustrates the personnel requirements for the basic units: the Senior Headquarters, the Regional Office, and the Inspection Echelons for monitoring allowed production of declared facilities, and the pools. The major roles of the Senior Headquarters and Regional Offices are to serve as communication channels from the inspecting teams to their respective sponsors and to provide administrative and logistical services. The duties of the personnel are self-explanatory.

Table 3–2 reflects the deployment of the basic units shown in Table 3–1 on the assumption of one Senior Headquarters, ten Regional Offices,[10] one hundred declared plants requiring inspection, and an undetermined

TABLE 3–1. Unit Personnel Reference Data (hypothetical organization)*

Note**	I Mixed System with Reciprocal and International Elements with Own Respective Organic Support[1]			II Mixed System with Support[1] for International Org'n Provided by Reciprocal Organization		
	Senior Hqtrs.	Regional Office	Inspection Echelon	Senior Hqtrs.[3]	Regional Office[3]	Inspection Echelon
Supervisor	1 (1)	1 (1)		1 (1)	1 (1)	
Assistants	5 (1)	1 (1)		5 (1)	1 (1)	
Legal	1 (1)			1 (1)		
Clerical	4 (2)	2 (1)		4 (2)	2 (1)	
Communication	16 (16)	4 (4)		16	4	
Transportation						
Aviation	4 (4)	4 (4)		4	4	
Motor	13 (8)	13 (8)		16	16	
Supply	2 (2)			2 (1)		
Purchasing	1 (1)			1		
Finance	1 (1)			1 (1)		
Interpreters	2 (1)	1 (1)		2 (1)	1 (1)	
Security	8 (8)	5 (5)		8	5	
Medical	1 (1)	1 (1)		1 (1)	1 (1)	
Sub-Totals	59 (47)	32 (26)		62 (9)	35 (5)	
Inspectors						
Plant (per shift)[4]			2 (1)			2 (1)
Pool			50 (10)			50 (10)
20% Non-Available Factor[5]	12 (10)	6 (5)		12 (2)	7 (1)	
Total	71 (57)	38 (31)		74 (11)	42 (6)	

Note**	III Mixed System with Support[1] for Reciprocal Organization Provided by International Organization			IV Host Country Providing Support[1] for Both Reciprocal and International Organization		
	Senior Hqtrs.[3]	Regional Office[3]	Inspection Echelon	Senior Hqtrs.	Regional Office	Inspection Echelon
Supervisor	1 (1)	1 (1)		1 (1)	1 (1)	
Assistants	5 (1)	1 (1)		5 (1)	1 (1)	
Legal	1 (1)			1 (1)		
Clerical	4 (2)	2 (2)		4 (2)	2 (1)	
Communication	(16)	(4)		8[2] (8)[2]		
Transportation						
Aviation	(4)	(4)				
Motor	(16)	(16)				
Supply	1 (2)			2 (2)		
Purchasing	(1)			1 (1)		
Finance	1 (1)			1 (1)		
Interpreters	2 (1)	1 (1)		2 (1)	1 (1)	
Security	(8)	(5)		8 (8)	5 (5)	
Medical	1 (1)	1 (1)		1 (1)	1 (1)	
Sub-Totals	16 (55)	6 (35)		34 (27)	11 (10)	
Inspectors						
Plant (per shift)[4]			2 (1)			2 (1)
Pool			50 (10)			50 (10)
20% Non-Available Factor[5]	3 (11)	1 (7)		7 (5)	2 (2)	
Total	19 (66)	7 (42)		41 (32)	13 (12)	

* It is not unlikely that, as sensor technology proceeds, the number of personnel required for inspection might be reduced.

** Reciprocal elements without parentheses; international elements with parentheses.

[1] Support—communications and transportation internal in Host Country.

[2] Communications from senior Hqtrs. to sponsor external to Host Country.

[3] Offices occupied jointly.

[4] Refers to operating 8-hour shifts at declared plants conducting allowed production of affected items.

[5] Factor for leaves, sick, etc.

TABLE 3–2. Hypothetical Inspection Organization (in a host country)

	I Mixed System with Reciprocal and International Elements Providing Own Respective Organic Support			II Mixed System with Support for International Org'n Provided by Reciprocal Organization[2]		
	[1]1 shift	2 shifts	3 shifts	1 shift	2 shifts	3 shifts
Senior Hqtrs.	71 (57)	71 (57)	71 (57)	74 (11)	74 (11)	74 (11)
10 Regional Offices	380 (310)	380 (310)	380 (310)	420 (60)	420 (60)	420 (60)
Inspectors						
100 Plants (declared)	200 (100)	400 (200)	600 (300)	200 (100)	400 (200)	600 (300
Pool	50 (10)	50 (10)	50 (10)	50 (10)	50 (10)	50 (10)
20% Non-Available						
Factor	50 (22)	90 (42)	130 (62)	50 (22)	90 (42)	130 (62)
Total	751 (499)	991 (619)	1231 (739)	794 (203)	1034 (323)	1274 (443)
Grand Total Mixed System	1250	1610	1970	997	1357	1717

	III Mixed System with Support for Reciprocal Org'n Provided by International Organization[2]			IV Mixed System with Host Country Providing Support for both Reciprocal and International Organization		
	1 shift	2 shifts	3 shifts	1 shift	2 shifts	3 shifts
Senior Hqtrs.	19 (66)	19 (66)	19 (66)	41 (32)	41 (32)	41 (32)
10 Regional Offices	70 (420)	70 (420)	70 (420)	130 (120)	130 (120)	130 (120)
Inspectors						
100 Plants (declared)	200 (100)	400 (200)	600 (300)	200 (100)	400 (200)	600 (300)
Pool	50 (10)	50 (10)	50 (10)	50 (10)	50 (10)	50 (10)
20% Non-Available						
Factor	50 (22)	90 (42)	130 (62)	50 (22)	90 (42)	130 (62)
Total	389 (618)	629 (738)	869 (858)	471 (284)	711 (404)	951 (524)
Grand Total Mixed System	1007	1367	1727	755	1115	1475

[1] Shifts refer primarily to operating shifts at plants.
[2] Offices jointly occupied.
ASSUMPTIONS:
  Mission: To inspect 100 plants and execute functions related to a freeze treaty.
  Composition: 1 Senior Hqtrs., 10 Regional Offices, Inspection Personnel for 100 plants and related functions. Figures without parentheses denote reciprocal personnel. Figures with parentheses denote international personnel.
  Concept of Employment: Reciprocal Personnel strengths reflect personnel of one signatory nation or from several signatory nations on a pooling concept. If pooling is not employed, there could be several reciprocal organizations of varying composition depending upon the desires of the respective inspecting nations. In a mixed system, the international elements operate in coordination with the reciprocal inspecting organization and the host country.

quantity of inspections of undeclared production facilities, observations of space launchings and missile firings, verifications of destruction and accidental losses of strategic nuclear delivery vehicles and launchers, checks of declared facilities no longer producing affected items, and tasks related to the limitation of launchers.

CONCLUSION

A verification system for a freeze proposal based on the reciprocal concept would be practicable when not more than five states were actively involved. As the number of states increased, recourse should be had to various types of pooling arrangements. Adoption of a mixed system would be advisable in order to accord greater credibility to the data reported, give wider publicity to verification and arms control, enlarge the number of participating states, and provide individuals of other nations with the training and experience necessary to staff future international arms control bodies.

The organizational structures analyzed in connection with the U.S. freeze proposal possess varying degrees of effectiveness with regard to the confidence factor under the verification system. The differences relate primarily to the technical means of verification. Some modifications in organizational procedure, such as rotation of inspectors between assignments and frequent training exercises at their own research and production facilities, could help minimize such difficulties.

The verification technique contemplated is visual observation of gross external characteristics. It would, therefore, be essential that affected armaments, sub-assemblies, and other objects be easy to detect and identify. No unique or unusual equipment would be required for this, but adequate administration, communications, and transportation would be crucial. For an inspecting organization to carry out its mission, sufficient access and freedom of movement would have to be guaranteed.

The technical qualifications of the inspectors should be related to the tasks they perform. Inspectors assigned to production activities should be technicians qualified to verify the production aspects and characteristics of the specified items and sub-assemblies. Inspectors assigned to tasks other than production should possess a general knowledge of pertinent weapons components and terminology. An engineering background, oriented to either aircraft or missiles as required, with technical training in weapons familiarization would be advisable. In addition, proficiency in the language of the country in which the inspection was to be conducted would be desirable.

Under each organizational structure examined, the role of the inspector would be strictly limited to gathering and reporting data to the inspecting state or states. Determining whether a violation of the freeze agreement had been committed and the appropriate response to the violation would rest with the inspecting state and not with the inspectors.

PROPOSALS FOR STAGE I OF
GENERAL AND COMPLETE DISARMAMENT

On September 20, 1961, the United States and the Soviet Union joined forces to submit to the General Assembly of the United Nations a *Joint Statement of Agreed Principles for Disarmament Negotiations,* which the Assembly subsequently recommended as the basis for negotiations on GCD. The joint statement included the following: "To implement control over and inspection of disarmament, an International Disarmament Organization including all parties to the agreement should be created within the framework of the United Nations. This International Disarmament Organization and its inspectors should be assured unrestricted access without veto to all places as necessary for the purpose of effective verification." In order to reach agreement on this principle, the United States did not insist on inclusion of an explicit statement that verification "should ensure that not only agreed limitations or reductions take place but also that retained armed forces and armament do not exceed agreed levels at any stage." But the United States made clear that this was "a key element" in its position. The

Soviet Union replied that, "while strongly advocating effective control over disarmament," it was "resolutely opposed to the establishment of control over armaments." Throughout the negotiations this issue has remained the principal point of disagreement.

On April 18, 1962, the United States introduced in the ENDC its "Outline of Basic Provisions of a Treaty on General and Complete Disarmament in a Peaceful World." A month earlier the Soviet Union had submitted its "Draft Treaty on General and Complete Disarmament under Strict International Control." Both contain provisions for an International Disarmament Organization. The two drafts, modified in some particulars, have been the basis for discussions in the ENDC and the U.N. General Assembly on GCD.

The verification functions that IDO is expected to perform under both U.S. and Soviet proposals for GCD were discussed in considerable detail in the ENDC, but the provisions concerning the structure and powers of IDO were not. Therefore, in considering the problems that are likely to arise in reaching agreement on the establishment of IDO, this study draws heavily upon past experience with international organizations and past positions which the United States and the Soviet Union have taken.

The international organizational arrangements accepted in the past may not necessarily be appropriate for IDO, in view of the very broad scope of its mission. An organization to verify compliance with a treaty on GCD would be a vast undertaking, requiring very large numbers of highly qualified personnel. Moreover, it would be dealing with peculiarly sensitive matters that affect vital security interests of its members. Some departure from the principles, precedents, and cliches of the past may be necessary if an effective IDO is to be established.

It should also be noted that this study deals only with Stage I of the GCD proposal. Organizational arrangements for verifying compliance with the measures called for in Stage I would have serious implications for Stages II and III, and the conclusions here might have to be modified for later stages.

Role of an International Disarmament Organization

The United States proposal for Stage I of GCD encompasses six areas: reduction of armaments and limitations or prohibitions on the production and testing of armaments, reduction of armed forces, nuclear controls, outer space, military expenditures, and reduction of the risk of war.

The Soviet proposal, while covering many of the same areas, calls for more drastic reductions, limitations, and prohibitions. It also calls for the program to be carried out more rapidly than envisaged in the

U.S. proposal. These differences have implications for IDO primarily in terms of the size of the operation it would be expected to undertake.

Of greater significance for IDO is the disagreement between the United States and the Soviet Union concerning the responsibility of IDO to provide assurances that agreed limitations are not exceeded and that prohibited activities are not being conducted. The United States has stated that by "assurances" it means "reasonable or adequate assurance, not foolproof assurance—which is never attainable anyway."[1] Nevertheless, this requirement has major "quantitative" and "qualitative" implications for IDO. A large organization would be needed, and it would have to be able to carry out sophisticated and covert operations unusual for international bodies. Except on this question of IDO's responsibilities concerning clandestine activities and stockpiles of armaments, the U.S. and Soviet positions with regard to the functions of IDO do not appear to be far apart.

Reduction of Armaments. The U.S. proposal for Stage I calls for the following measures: 30 percent reduction of certain types of armaments, limitations on the production of such armaments, limitations on production facilities, prohibition of the production and testing of new types of armaments, limitations on the flight testing of missiles, and examination of questions related to the reduction and eventual elimination of chemical and biological weapons of mass destruction.

Under the U.S. proposal, "specified" parties to the Treaty would reduce by 30 percent their stocks of certain types of major armaments.[2] The proposal mentions various types of missiles, armed combat aircraft, combatant ships, artillery systems, tanks, armored cars, and personnel carriers. The United States explained that its proposal is designed to cover "all armaments the reduction of which it seems practicable to supervise." It has indicated a willingness to include other armaments if satisfactory verification systems can be worked out.

Within a specified time after the beginning of Stage I, the parties would submit to IDO a declaration of their inventories of the specified armaments. Reductions would take place in three steps, each divided into two parts of six months duration. During the first part of each step, the armaments to be reduced would be deposited in depots under IDO's supervision. During the second part, these armaments would be destroyed or converted to peaceful uses under IDO's supervision. There would submit to IDO a declaration of their inventories of the specified tions.

The Soviet proposal calls for the elimination of all nuclear weapons delivery systems, except that "an agreed and strictly limited number of intercontinental missiles, anti-missile missiles, and anti-aircraft missiles in the 'ground-to-air' category" are to be retained by the United

States and the Soviet Union "exclusively on their own territory" until the end of Stage III. The Soviet Union has never stated how many missiles the two powers should be permitted to retain. The Soviet proposal also calls for a thirty percent reduction in "conventional" armaments.

The United States has stated that it has no objection "in principle" to including measures for the reduction of conventional armaments in Stage I, but it has pointed out the difficulties of verifying reductions of light arms which can be easily concealed and manufactured in small factories. While doubting that it is worthwhile to burden IDO at the outset with this extra task, the United States has said that it is "open-minded" about extending the categories to be reduced in Stage I, *if* the Soviet Union would be prepared to accept the required verification procedures.

The differences in the two proposals as to the amounts and categories of armaments to be reduced during Stage I have implications for IDO primarily in terms of the size of the operation it would be expected to carry out. Of more direct significance is disagreement over the question of "retained weapons." The U.S. proposal calls on IDO not only to verify reductions but also to "provide assurance that retained armaments [do] not exceed agreed levels."

It is difficult to see how IDO could provide the required assurance unless it had complete access to, and freedom of movement within, the territories of all the states concerned. The United States has recognized this by suggesting the possibility of "only spot and random checking . . . for hidden armaments" which would involve a relatively small part of national territory.[3] It is in this connection that the idea of progressive "zonal" inspection has been put forward. The Soviet Union repeatedly maintains that IDO can only verify *reductions* in armaments and armed forces and that there can be no control over, or verification of, *retained* armaments and armed forces. In its view, this would be an "international system of legalized espionage."[4] The Soviet Union has made one concession on this point, however. If its proposal that the United States and the Soviet Union retain only a strictly limited number of missiles were accepted, the Soviet Union would agree to international "control over the remaining missiles at the launching pads."[5]

The U.S. proposal for limitations on the production of armaments differs from its proposal for armaments reduction in that the former would apply to *all* parties to the Treaty. The permitted production would be small. It would be limited to replacements for accidental losses, armaments expended in training, and armaments that have so deteriorated as to become inoperative. IDO would have to verify these depletions. Under the Soviet proposal, all facilities for the production of nuclear weapons delivery systems would be closed down or converted to peaceful purposes under the supervision of IDO. It would seem more logical to call for the cessation of all production, with replacements drawn from existing stocks. But the United States position is that "the dismantling of the industrialized base which underlies the production of armaments must be done gradually as confidence in the workability of the disarmament process increases."

Under the U.S. plan, "all facilities involved in the production of major armaments would be declared *in toto*," but inspectors would be stationed at, and have access to, only "relevant" production facilities. Again, the idea of progressive zonal inspection is suggested.

Any system established to verify the limitations on the production of armaments should be adequate for verifying other aspects of the U.S. proposal, such as the prohibition on the expansion or modernization of production facilities and on the production of new types of weapons. There would be room for judgment as to whether a particular modification of a plant or a weapons design constituted a violation of these prohibitions. But it is difficult to see how IDO could in all cases provide assurance that no party had tested a new weapon as the U.S. proposal requires.

The U.S. proposal calls for a limitation on the flight testing of missiles. Presumably, the permitted testing would be for confidence and training purposes, and IDO would need advance notification. Its inspectors would need the right to inspect the missiles thoroughly and keep them under constant surveillance until the firing.

Armed Forces. The armed forces of the United States and the Soviet Union would be limited under the U.S. proposal in Stage I to 2.1 million men. The Soviet Union proposes a ceiling of 1.9 million, which would include officers, enlisted men, and civilian employees. As for the other parties to the Treaty, the Soviet proposal states that agreed force levels would be included in the Treaty. The U.S. proposal provides that, with agreed exceptions, other parties would reduce their force levels to 100,000 or 1 percent of their population, whichever is higher.

The method for reducing armed forces under the U.S. proposal is similar to that proposed for the reduction of armaments. IDO would verify the reductions and "provide assurance that retained forces did not exceed agreed levels." Reduction of forces under the Soviet proposal is linked to the removal of troops from foreign territories, the dismantling of foreign bases, and the elimination of nuclear weapons delivery systems.

Verification of the reduction of conventional armaments presents fewer problems than verification of military manpower reductions. Circumventions of manpower ceilings would be difficult to detect, but would not be of great importance in any event if the forces did not possess sufficient combat weapons and equipment.

Nuclear Controls. The following measures are included in Stage I of the U.S. proposal: prohibition on the production of fissionable materials for use in nuclear weapons; limitations on the production of such materials for other purposes; transfer of such materials to other states for peaceful purposes only; transfer by the United States and the Soviet Union of specified "amounts" of weapons grade material to peaceful purposes; non-transfer and non-acquisition of nuclear weapons; prohibition of nuclear weapons tests: and examination of questions related to the reduction and elimination of nuclear weapons stockpiles.

The heart of the U.S. proposal concerning nuclear disarmament is the provision obligating each party to the Treaty to "halt, prohibit and prevent the production, at facilities under its jurisdiction and control, of fissionable materials for use in nuclear weapons." The purpose of this proposal is to ensure that future production of fissionable materials is used only for peaceful purposes. This is popularly known as the "cutoff." The requirements for verifying a cutoff have been discussed in considerable detail in connection with the U.S. proposal for a cutoff as a separate partial measure to be taken independently of and in advance of Stage I. This proposal is discussed separately in this volume and its conclusions will not be repeated here, beyond stating the principal one that the IAEA could assume the functions of verifying compliance with the cutoff and could provide reasonable assurances against violations.

Should an agreement for a cutoff be in effect at the time IDO was established and the verification arrangements were working satisfactorily, there might be no need to integrate the arrangements into IDO immediately. Eventually, however, IDO (or some international organization of a more limited nature established to verify a number of partial arms control measures) would take over the verification of the cutoff. This would be due partly to the disadvantages of having separate verification systems; also at some point, as the production of fissionable materials expands, the general structure of the IAEA would be inadequate for carrying out the verification of the cutoff. Should there be no agreement on a cutoff prior to the initiation of Stage I, IDO would have to develop its own verification machinery.

A system set up to verify compliance with a cutoff could also verify that agreed limitations on the production of fissionable materials were being observed. It could verify the proposed prohibition on the transfer of fissionable materials to other states for use in nuclear weapons insofar as those transfers were declared. Furthermore, the arrangements for verifying the cutoff would be adequate for any functions IDO might have to undertake in connection with the proposal that the United States and the Soviet Union transfer to IDO depots specified amounts of weapons grade material at the beginning of Stage I.[6]

The U.S. proposal to prevent additional national nuclear forces is two fold. Those parties that have manufactured nuclear weapons would agree not to "transfer control" of such weapons to a state which had not manufactured them before an agreed date and not to assist such states in their manufacture. On the other hand, the "non-nuclear" states would agree not "to acquire or attempt to acquire control" over any such weapons and not to manufacture or attempt to manufacture any nuclear weapons. The Soviet proposal is similar to that of the United States, except for an additional provision by which states not possessing such weapons would not permit nuclear weapons of other states into their territories.

A system to verify the cutoff would curb the independent manufacture of nuclear weapons by non-nuclear parties to the Treaty. The draft non-proliferation treaty jointly tabled by the U.S. and the Soviet Union in March 1968 would have a similar effect and would also prohibit the transfer of nuclear weapons to such states.

Under the U.S. proposal, all parties would agree to be bound by a treaty banning nuclear weapons tests in all environments; the Soviet proposal calls for a prohibition on the conduct of "nuclear tests of any kind." The Limited Test Ban Treaty of August 5, 1963, already prohibits the testing of nuclear weapons in the atmosphere, outer space, and underwater. It proved impossible to reach agreement banning underground testing, because of the differences between the Soviet Union and the United States over the need for on-site inspections. Presumably, arrangements for verifying such a ban would eventually be incorporated in IDO.

The U.S. Stage I proposals do not call for any reduction of nuclear weapons or any inspection of facilities for their storage or fabrication. The parties would agree "to examine unresolved questions related to the means of accomplishing in Stages II and III the reduction and eventual elimination of nuclear weapons stockpiles, and, in the light of this examination, shall agree upon arrangements for the accomplishment of such reduction and elimination." The United States hopes that this study could commence immediately so that there would be "no remaining questions" by the time Stage I began. The Soviet Union has also proposed the elimination of stockpiles at Stage II, but has indicated a willingness to transfer this measure to Stage I.

Outer Space. With regard to outer space, the U.S. proposal contains the following provisions: prohibition on the placing of weapons for mass destruction in orbit; advance notification and pre-launch inspection of space vehicles and missiles; limitations on the production, stock-piling, and testing of boosters for space vehicles; and increased international cooperation in the peaceful uses of outer space.

The ban on orbiting weapons of mass destruction, which is also included in the Soviet proposal for Stage I, has already been incorporated in the Outer Space Treaty of January 27, 1967. The treaty does not, however, contain international arrangements for verifying compliance with this prohibition similar to those included in the proposals for Stage I of GCD.

To police this prohibition, both the United States and Soviet Union proposals provided for pre-launch inspection by IDO of all space vehicles and missiles. The procedure would be essentially the same as that for flight testing of missiles. The United States proposes that IDO "establish and operate any arrangements necessary for detecting unreported launchings" and has suggested "a network of ground-based and possibly space-borne instruments."[7]

As for the production and testing of boosters the system would be generally the same as that for missiles. There would be one important difference, however; a primary purpose in inspecting missiles is to ascertain that there have been no improvements in their design. This prohibition would not be applicable in the case of space vehicles, for there is no intent to impede their development. Thorough inspection would provide all parties with complete information as to scientific or technological advances.

With regard to clandestine production, it has been suggested that since "the body of the rocket . . . would be difficult to disguise" and final assembly would require "unique facilities," such production "subsequent to the implementation of a disarmament treaty could—given suitable inspection—be less of a danger than clandestine storage of previous production."[8] Normally, neither the United States nor the Soviet Union would maintain large stockpiles of boosters, although as the pace of space activities increases there would be more to account for. Since these boosters can be easily converted to weapons uses, it would be necessary to keep a strict account of their numbers and locations. There would seem to be no way of verifying with a high degree of assurance that parties have not stockpiled boosters prior to the initiation of the system, but they should be required at the outset to declare their inventories and related facilities.

With regard to "increased international cooperation in peaceful uses of outer space in the United Nations or through other appropriate arrangements," the United Kingdom has suggested the possibility of internationalizing "the whole of space research," but this does not seem feasible at present. Nonetheless it would be "highly desirable that all space projects be brought as soon as possible under some comprehensive organization for international collaboration."[9] IDO might well be the appropriate agency for supervising such a program.

Military Expenditures. The U.S. proposal does not expressly include the reduction of military expenditures as a measure to be carried out during Stage I. It states that such reductions would be "inevitable" under its proposals. The United States maintains that "budgetary limitations" are "not in themselves a useful means of bringing disarmament about" and has pointed out that "the extremely diverse national systems of budgeting do not readily lend themselves to comparability or to standardized definitions and procedures of control."[10]

The United States does propose that itemized reports on military expenditures be submitted to IDO and calls for an examination of "questions related to the verifiable reduction of military expenditures." While "pessimistic about the feasibility of military expenditure reduction as a substantive disarmament measure," the United States has been "more optimistic about the possibilities of utilizing military expenditures as one of the techniques for verification."

The Soviet Union includes reduction of military expenditures in its Stage I proposal and proposes a freeze or a percentage reduction of military budgets as a measure which could be taken prior to Stage I. This proposal has received a generally favorable response in the ENDC. Whether or not such reductions are included as measures to be taken in Stage I, the duties of IDO would undoubtedly include the inspection of records on military budgets and expenditures.

Reduction of the Risk of War. "In order to promote confidence and reduce the risk of war," the U.S. proposal for Stage I calls for agreement on the following measures: advance notification of military movements and maneuvers which would include maneuvers of ground forces, naval surface forces of substantial size, co-ordinated flights of sizable numbers of military aircraft, and launching of an unusual number of long-range ballistic missiles; establishment of observation posts at major ports, railway centers, motor highways, river crossings and air bases; "additional observation arrangements" such as aerial observation, mobile ground observation teams, and overlapping radars; exchange of military missions; establishment of rapid and reliable communications among heads of governments and with the U.N. Secretary General; and a study of possible further measures for reducing the risk of war.

Within the ENDC, these measures have been discussed as "partial" measures which might be taken before the initiation of Stage I. They have been considered almost exclusively within the context of agreements between the Warsaw Pact countries and the members of NATO and CENTO, to be carried out on a "reciprocal" basis. There has been little mention of the possible role of IDO in this connection.

IDO would receive notification of military movements and maneuvers. It could attach its own observers to the observation posts, any additional observation arrangements, and military missions. If such arrangements were established in a number of areas, IDO could perform a useful clearinghouse function as well as help to establish standards and ground rules. Finally, under the U.S. proposal the study of possible further measures for reducing the risk of war would be carried out by a subsidiary organ of IDO.

The Soviet proposal calls for notification to IDO of military movements, bans "large-scale joint maneuvers," and restricts the movement of military forces, warships, and military aircraft to their own territories. The Soviet Union has indicated that it might consider the establishment of observation posts and exchange of military missions if certain conditions were met, e.g., the denuclearization and thinning out of military forces in Central Europe.

Structure and Powers of an International Disarmament Organization

The U.S. and Soviet proposals with regard to an IDO contain similar provisions but differ on a number of key points. Neither proposal can be considered to be a complete blueprint. The Soviet proposal is more detailed, but unclear on some important points. The U.S. proposal is an "outline" which does not purport to be complete and does not deal with a number of crucial issues. Since the two proposals have not been discussed in the ENDC or the United Nations and have not been the subject of comment by responsible officials, it is difficult to determine the extent of the similarities and differences. For this reason, the following analysis of the structure and powers of IDO draws heavily on the experiences of other international organizations, the past positions taken by the major powers, and past proposals regarding organizational arrangements.

The scope of this study does not allow for a detailed analysis of the whole range of possible organizational and procedural arrangements for Stage I. Instead, it focuses on those issues which are likely to be the most difficult and most important to resolve before any agreement could be reached for establishing an IDO.

Membership. Participation of all militarily significant states would be essential for the continuing effectiveness of the Treaty and for the coming into force of particular measures or stages. This principle is recognized in the U.S. proposal which, however, provides that the Treaty would be open to "all members of the United Nations or its specialized agencies." In existing circumstances, Communist China, East Germany, North Korea, and North Vietnam would be excluded.

For Stage I, it would not be necessary to include smaller states having few armaments. Their participation could be a complicating factor and divert energies from the essential task of bringing under control the armaments of states with substantial inventories of sophisticated weapons. Nonetheless, for political reasons, membership in IDO should be open to all states. Eventually it would be desirable for all to join.

Admission to IDO should be made as easy as possible. Decisions should be based on the ability and willingness of a state to carry out its obligations. Approval of applicants by a simple majority vote in the General Conference and the Control Council of IDO would seem to be the appropriate procedure.

The practice of international organizations with regard to withdrawal varies. Many statutes of specialized agencies provide for withdrawal. The U.N. Charter is silent on this question, although the right of a member to withdraw in certain circumstances was recognized at the San Francisco Conference.

Any state determined to withdraw would not be inhibited in any event. It would seem necessary to make some arrangement for the possible application of sanctions, either through IDO or through recourse to the United Nations, if the withdrawal of a state were followed by actions that endangered the disarmament program. As a practical matter, sanctions could not be imposed on the major military powers. Should one of them withdraw from IDO, the treaty would in all probability collapse.

The growth of international organizations has fostered a "tendency within the law of nations toward acceptance of a paramount community interest, especially with regard to matters of international security."[11] This was the basis for conferring upon the United Nations in Article 2(6) the obligation to ensure that non-members of the organization act in accordance with the principles of the Charter "so far as may be necessary for the maintenance of international peace and security." It would seem appropriate to confer a similar authority on IDO.

The General Conference. Every international organization has one body in which all members are represented. Such an organ is provided for in the U.S. and Soviet proposals for IDO. It is in the interest of the United States to restrict the powers of the General Conference to a minimum. If IDO is to be an effective organization, the locus of power must be the Control Council, and the Conference cannot be permitted to interfere with its operations.

Both the U.S. and the Soviet proposals establish the predominance of the Council over the Conference. Under the U.S. proposal, the main function of the Conference would be to approve decisions previously agreed upon in the Council, such as appointment of the Administrator, approval of the budget, and accessions to the Treaty. The Conference could request and receive reports from the Council, propose matters for consideration by the Council, and "decide" upon matters so referred to it. The Conference would be empowered to consider "matters of mutual interests pertaining to the Treaty or disarmament in general," but the U.S. proposal does not authorize the Conference to make recommendations on such matters. It is not unusual for pressures to build up (particularly from the smaller states not guaranteed representation on the executive organ) to increase the powers of the plenary organ. This would probably be the case with regard to IDO. The Soviet proposal for an IDO provides for recommendations by the Conference to the parties and to the Council, but the U.S. proposal does not.

The deliberations of the General Conference of IDO would probably be dominated by extraneous political considerations. It would be desirable that the powers of the General Conference be so restricted that they do not interfere with the functions of the Control Council, for the Conference could easily become a forum for exerting pressure for a more rapid implementation of GCD than prudence would dictate. Despite these arguments for limiting the powers of the General Conference, it would probably be necessary to confer on the Conference general powers to make recommendations to the Council, as the Soviet proposal provides.

Given the limited functions of the Conference, annual meetings might not be required, especially if provision is made for special sessions. Nonetheless, for political reasons, it would probably be desirable.

With regard to voting procedure, a system of "weighted" voting does not appear feasible. In the past the United States has favored a two-thirds vote for certain important categories of decisions as a means of protecting itself from costly programs for which it would bear the largest financial burden. The possibility seems remote that the General Conference, with its limited powers, could embark on far-reaching programs which the United States did not approve. Rather the danger lies in the possibility that the Conference might frustrate the operations of the Organization by refusing to adopt the budget. Voting by a simple majority would be preferable, but it may not be possible to reach agreement on the point. The Soviet proposal, which calls for a two-thirds vote on all but procedural matters, would provide numerous opportunities for a minority of members to paralyze operations. If it is necessary to specify that some decisions require a two-thirds vote, it would be in the interests of the United States to restrict the list to a minimum.

The Control Council. The successful implementation of GCD would be dependent upon the effective operation of the Control Council of

IDO. Ideally, it should be a small body, composed primarily of the military powers. It should be an "executive" body. It must be a "working" organ, not a propaganda platform, and it must have the powers necessary for effective supervision.

In determining the size of such an organ it is necessary to balance two principles: first, the body must not be so large as to be unwieldy; and second, it must be large enough to afford representation to the major interest groups. The size of the IDO Council would be related to the size of IDO itself. If IDO had the same membership as the United Nations, it is difficult to see how a council smaller than the ENDC[12] could meet the demands of various groups for representation.[13] If many smaller states are not initially members of IDO, a small Council would be preferable in the expectation that there would be strong pressure for enlarging it as more states joined. This has happened in almost all cases in recent years.

Given the nature of the functions of IDO, the major powers are not likely to leave the selection of the Council entirely in the hands of the General Conference. Both the U.S. and Soviet proposals provide for "permanent" and "nonpermanent" membership. Under the Soviet proposal, the states permanently represented on the IDO Council would be the same as those on the U.N. Security Council. The U.S. proposal states that the Council shall consist of "all the major signatory powers" and "certain other parties to the Treaty on a rotating basis." Presumably this would mean permanent membership for the militarily significant states. Should any of these states not be parties to the Treaty from the outset, as for example China, provision should be made for subsequently giving them permanent representation.

The U.S. proposal lays down no criteria for the selection of the other members of the Council, but the Soviet proposal stipulates that "the composition of the Council must ensure proper representation of the three principal groups of States existing in the world." In effect the Western powers have conceded to the Soviet demand for "parity" of representation of both sides in the disarmament negotiations, but have consistently opposed Soviet insistence that the world should be divided into three parts.

While the Soviet proposal for equitable "ideological" distribution of the seats on the IDO Control Council is unacceptable, the principle of "equitable geographical distribution" would have to be given some recognition. This principle has become embedded in international organizations. On the basis of past experience, it is likely that there will be pressures to increase the size of the Council and to provide assurances as to how the seats will be distributed.

Ideally, the criteria for selecting members of the IDO Council should balance the geographical distribution principle with recognition of the capacities of states to contribute to the successful implementation of the program. Past experience indicates that it is difficult to devise a formula to meet these criteria.

The importance of the voting procedure in the Council is obvious. The U.S. proposal is silent on the question of voting procedure, while the Soviet Union proposes that decisions, other than those on "procedural" matters, require a two-thirds vote in the Council. The Soviet representative in the ENDC has stated that there is "no need to introduce the principle of unanimity or the 'veto' " into the IDO Council.[14] However, if the Council is to be divided into three equal groups of representatives as the Soviets propose, each group would need only a single additional vote in order to veto any action.

The Soviet proposal would be unacceptable if the Soviet Union, its allies, and one or two other members could block operations. From this point of view, it would be in the interest of the United States for decisions of the Council to be taken by a simple majority. On the other hand, the United States has an interest in stemming any move for more rapid implementation of the disarmament program than prudence dictates. On balance, it would seem more desirable for the United States to support a major power veto or a two-thirds vote on a strictly limited range of decisions than to accept any voting procedure of the Control Council which might paralyze the Organization.

Both the United States and the Soviet Union propose to make the Council the predominant organ within IDO. However, its powers would be less than those of the U.N. Security Council. The functions of the IDO Council would be circumscribed by other provisions of the Treaty, especially the important provisions concerning verification. Moreover, the Council apparently would not have authority to "enforce" its decisions, as does the U.N. Security Council.

Among the functions assigned to the Control Council under the U.S. proposal are: adopt rules for implementing the Treaty; establish procedures and standards for the installation and operation of the verification arrangements and supervise such arrangements; recommend the budget; transmit reports to the United Nations; recommend the appointment of the Administrator, supervise his operations, and consider his reports on the verification arrangements; recommend accessions to the Treaty; and request advisory opinions from the International Court of Justice.

The Control Council would also establish "procedures for making available to the Parties to the Treaty data produced by verification arrangements." This would provide the basis for a public airing of any charges that parties were not fulfilling their obligations and give members the information necessary to decide what, if any, response they might wish to make in the event of violation of the Treaty.

Under the U.S. proposal the Control Council would "consider matters of mutual interest pertaining to the Treaty or to disarmament in general," but nothing is said about the measures the Council may take in this connection. It is doubtful that the Council could exercise any real control unless it had the power to make recommendations to the parties to the Treaty and perhaps to the United Nations as well. It would seem necessary to give the Council some general grant of authority, possibly including a general power of investigation and recommendation.

The U.S. proposal does not specifically authorize the Council to consider disputes that might arise in connection with the implementation of GCD. This power is implied in the general provisions regarding "disputes concerning the interpretation or application" of the Treaty. It would be advisable to permit the Council to consider such disputes and attempt to adjust them.

The U.S. proposal is silent regarding the handling of violations of the Treaty, and its views on this crucial issue have never been stated. By contrast, the Soviet position on this point is relatively clear. Under its proposal, the IDO Council would be required to "promptly notify" the U.N. Security Council "of any infringements by the States parties to the Treaty of their disarmament obligations under the present Treaty." In the ENDC, the Soviet representative has emphasized that the function of IDO is "to establish facts." It cannot be "entrusted with any functions involving preventive or enforcement measures against States." Measures to safeguard international peace and security are matters exclusively for the U.N. Security Council. The U.S. proposal does not preclude reporting violations to the U.N. Security Council, but it is questionable whether this would be an appropriate action in all cases, especially if the infringements were only minor. In the past, arms control proposals have suggested that the control organ have authority to impose certain sanctions in all cases short of the use of military force. It would not be easy to work out an agreement empowering the Control Council of IDO to impose even limited sanctions, but without such power it would be difficult for the Council to operate effectively.

In the event of a violation by a major military power, the decision as to the appropriate response would rest with the other major powers. The response might be limited to a declaration suspending or abrogating the treaty provision that had been violated. In all likelihood, a material violation would bring about dissolution of the Organization, a step that might be accompanied by a decision to exercise the right of individual or collective self-defense under Article 51 of the U.N. Charter.

The Administrator. The U.S. proposal provides for an Administrator to be appointed by the General Conference on the recommendation of the Control Council and to administer IDO "under the direction of the Control Council." The Soviet proposal contains no provision for an Administrator and assigns to the Council a number of functions normally carried out by the chief administrative officer of an international organization (e.g., preparing the budget, recruiting the staff, etc.).

The Soviet Union is likely to support a three member administrative council, each member representing one of the three principal groups of states. Considering strong Western opposition to this "troika" concept, the Soviet Union may not press this point except in connection with the control of international armed forces. But Soviet agreement to a single Administrator would probably require concessions concerning his appointment and functions and the organization of the staff. The Soviet Union would probably insist on assurances regarding the distribution of the top positions in IDO. Other groups would seek similar assurances. This problem has continually plagued the United Nations.

The experience of the United Nations argues against a veto over the appointment of a chief administrative officer. But the IDO Administrator could not operate effectively if he were not acceptable to the major powers. One way to minimize the problem might be to name the first Administrator in the Treaty and provide for overlapping terms for the Administrator and the Deputy Administrator so that the Organization would still have a chief officer if difficulties arose over the reappointment of the Administrator or the appointment of his successor.

It would be preferable not to stipulate the Administrator's term of office in the Treaty itself. If it is necessary to do so, there are compelling reasons for giving him as long a term as possible. It would be undesirable to change Administrators during Stage I of the Treaty.

The United States envisages an IDO Administrator with strictly limited functions which would be basically "administrative," not "political." He would be the chief executive officer of the Organization. He would prepare the budget and recruit and supervise the staff. He would make reports to the Control Council "on the progress of disarmament measures and of their verification and on the installation and operation of the verification arrangements." He would administer the installation and operation of those arrangements, but the procedures and standards for them would be established by the Council which would maintain "supervision over such arrangements and the Administrator." In addition, the Administrator would make "available to the Parties to the Treaty data produced by the verification arrangements." His role would not be comparable to that of the U.N. Secretary-General. He would work under closer supervision by the Council than is usually the case in international bodies.

The Soviet Union is unlikely to agree to a single chief administrative officer for IDO unless his functions are restricted to housekeeping duties. If the position the Soviet Union took during the test ban negotiations is any guide, the IDO Administrator could "be entrusted with carrying out measures decided on in advance" by the Council but could not "take decisions automatically on the basis of certain criteria laid down for him."[15]

The Soviet Union considers that the Council itself should control the day-to-day operations of the Organization. The possibilities for obstruction are so great that it seems unlikely such a system could work for so delicate a task as verifying a Treaty for GCD. An operation as extensive as that envisaged for IDO is likely to be effective only upon the basis of routine procedures with centralized administrative direction under guidelines established and generally supervised by the political control organ.

The Staff. Reaching agreement on the staffing of IDO will be among the most difficult problems to arise during the negotiations. The U.S. proposal states that the Administrator would have staff "adequate to ensure effective and impartial implementation of the functions" of IDO. Since the United States has been a strong advocate of the concept of an international civil service, one may assume that it would favor staffing IDO on this basis. It should be recognized, however, that the nature of the national interests in IDO would be such that it would be necessary at least in the initial stages to give members, especially the major military powers, a greater voice in the selection of staff than is customary.

The heart of the concept of an international civil service is the provision embodied in the Charter and the statutes of all U.N. agencies that the staff "shall not seek or receive instructions from any source external" to the organization and that the members "shall not seek to influence them in the discharge of their duties." This concept is by no means universally understood or accepted. The Soviet Union's view is that an impartial international civil service is impossible to achieve and that international organizations should be staffed along quite different lines. It proposes that IDO be staffed "on an international basis so as to ensure that the three principal groups of States existing in the world are adequately represented." The Council is to recruit the staff "from among persons recommended by Governments."

The idea that the Control Council should itself recruit staff is unique, but there would be nothing extraordinary in the Council's approving major appointments. The proposition that staff members be "recommended" by governments is compatible with the concept of an international civil service, so long as the Organization is free to accept or reject the recommendation.

IDO would face a formidable task in recruiting the vast array of specialized personnel required to carry out its functions. They would be available from the major industrial nations, but in most other countries the supply is limited and the personnel are needed for domestic development programs. Many of IDO's functions would be so sensitive that it could not operate effectively with second or third rate personnel. Nonetheless, the principle of "geographical distribution" has become so firmly entrenched that its supporters would be likely to insist upon its inclusion in IDO's Statute. This could present real problems for IDO. It would be essential to insist that the "paramount consideration" is that the selection of staff meet the highest standards of efficiency, technical competence, and integrity.

Within international bodies, there has been increasing resort to the practice of "secondment," i.e., the appointment of persons for short periods who return to their national services at the end of their term. This practice has been defended primarily on the grounds that it permits the temporary employment of qualified personnel that might not otherwise be available to the Organization. This point is valid only insofar as governments are willing to take the necessary steps to make the personnel available. The practice has disadvantages: it impedes the development of a career service, it creates two classes of staff members with some friction between them, and it results in a constant turnover which makes for inefficiency. Moreover, personnel expecting to return to their national service may find it difficult to view international interests as paramount. Most important, it takes time to adapt to the international arena, and personnel often leave at the point when they are beginning to make a contribution.

Despite these drawbacks, IDO in its initial stages would have to depend heavily on personnel lent to it. This would require IDO to establish far more extensive in-service training programs and more effective liaison arrangements with governments.

The staffing of inspection teams would raise more difficult issues than the recruitment of a general secretariat. These teams would be the very heart of the system. It would be impossible for IDO to carry out its mandate unless they functioned effectively and members had confidence that they were doing so. Throughout the history of negotiations on disarmament, there has been some recognition that the general principles applicable to staffing might need to be modified with regard to inspection teams.[16]

If the idea were accepted that an international verification system could include "national" inspectors or observers, serving the interests of their own countries, various kinds of arrangements would be possible:

Reciprocal systems by which the inspection of one country or group of countries could be carried out by another and vice versa: the inspectors to be chosen by, and responsible to, their own governments.

Reciprocal systems plus international observers which would operate in much the same manner as the above system except that IDO inspectors would be attached to the teams to report their own findings to IDO and through IDO to all parties to the Treaty.

Reciprocal/international systems which could be composed of various mixtures of international and national elements.

International systems plus national observers under which inspection would be carried out by personnel selected by IDO and functioning under its direction with "national" observers attached to the teams to assure that the inspections were being conducted effectively.

International systems under which all inspectors would be selected by, responsible to, and report to the international organization alone.

Which system would be most appropriate for various types of disarmament measures would depend upon a number of factors: the sensitivity of the operations, the number of states directly involved, and the technical capabilities of IDO. Moreover, it should be possible to move from essentially reciprocal systems to an international system as confidence was built up and the capabilities of the organization increased.

There are a number of general principles that would have to be observed:

No national should be permitted, or expected, to serve on any team inspecting his own country, except in a liaison capacity.

In any mixed team of inspectors, the lines of command and control should be clearly established.

Under any system, there must be rapid and reliable means of communication and clearly defined rights of access and freedom of movement.

International inspectors or observers must be free at all times to communicate directly to IDO, and IDO would be under the obligation to make available to all parties all data produced by the verification system.

National inspectors serving on mixed teams or as observers might or might not be considered as part of the IDO staff, but they would *not* be considered part of the "international civil service" and would not be required to take the oath of loyalty to the Organization.

Under any system, it would be essential that each inspector be free to make his own report, for the obvious benefits of an agreed report should not be allowed to undermine the need for all countries to feel confident that they were getting all relevant information.

While IDO should take into account the legitimate concerns of the host country and other interested parties, decisions regarding its own personnel serving on inspection teams should rest with the Organization.

Financial Questions. The operation of IDO would very likely be the most costly ever undertaken by an international organization. The United States and other major powers would have to underwrite a substantially larger proportion of the costs than they now do under the U.N. scale of assessments.

Under the U.S. proposal, the scale of assessments would be set by the General Conference. The Soviet Union proposes that the "agreed scale of contributions" be included in the Treaty itself. It would be undesirable to freeze the scale of assessments by including it in the Treaty for this would introduce inflexibility that would be difficult to work with. A concession on this point may be necessary with regard to the initial budget, with the Conference authorized to revise the scale subsequently.

The U.S. and Soviet proposals call for consideration of the budget by the Council and the Conference. This raises the question of the appropriate voting procedure in the two organs. To permit a veto of individual items in the IDO budget would subject the Organization to many of the uncertainties that have plagued international programs financed on a voluntary basis. Nonetheless, as recent U.N. experience demonstrates, contributions must be assessed through a procedure best calculated to command the support of the principal contributors.

It would seem appropriate that the initial costs of installing the system be met largely by the major powers. The Soviet Union has repeatedly stated a preference for "equality" of contributions by the major powers. If this proposal were accepted, it should be made clear that it does not apply to "voluntary" contributions. Should the United States at some point wish to donate to IDO devices which it felt would improve the quality of inspection, it should not be precluded from doing so because of Soviet unwillingness to make a similar contribution. It should be remembered that during the discussion in the U.N. Military Staff Committee one way in which the Soviet Union sought to limit the size of the armed forces to be made available to the Security Council was by insisting that the contributions by each of the permanent members be equal in every respect.

Adoption of the budget is one area in which a veto by the major powers or a two-thirds voting requirement in the Control Council could be justified. The United States has tended to support a two-thirds voting requirement on financial questions in order to protect itself against the adoption of costly programs of which it did not approve. In IDO, the greater risk might well be the refusal of members to vote the necessary funds. It would not be in the interests of either the United States or the Soviet Union to permit a minority of small powers to frustrate IDO by refusing to adopt the budget. Therefore, it would seem appropriate for the Conference to approve the budget by a simple majority vote. Any Conference changes in the budget should require a two-thirds vote and approval by the Control Council.

IDO should be empowered to penalize members that fail to pay, or pay promptly, their assessments. But experience in the United Nations does not augur well for an agreement to include such a provision in the IDO Statute.

Privileges and Immunities. The principles governing the privileges and immunities of international organizations, their personnel, and the representatives are by now well established. With regard to IDO, it should not be difficult to work out acceptable arrangements along the lines of the agreement reached during the negotiations on a test ban treaty.[17] Some problems might arise with regard to inspection teams. The key issue is to balance the legitimate rights of states to protect themselves from excessively intrusive inspections against the needs of the inspection teams for clear, defined rights of access, communication, and freedom of movement.

Amendments. Statutes of international organizations differ from most multilateral treaties in that a qualified majority of members may adopt amendments that are binding upon all. With regard to a Treaty for GDC neither the United States nor the Soviet Union would be willing

99

to accept a Treaty so intimately related to its national security which could be amended without its consent. Any procedure for amendment of the IDO Statute would have to provide, as does the U.N. Charter, for approval and ratification by the major powers. Usually, amendments of the statutes of international bodies require adoption and ratification by two-thirds of the members. This procedure would seem appropriate in this case.

Relations with the United Nations. The United States and the Soviet Union are agreed that IDO should be established "within the framework of the United Nations." This vague term permits a wide range of possible relationships.

The U.S. proposal calls for an agreement between IDO and the United Nations and for reports by IDO to the U.N. General Assembly and Security Council. The "principal organs" of the United Nations could make recommendations to IDO which "would consider them and report to the United Nations on action taken." The U.S. proposal contains a note that it does not "cover all the possible details of aspects of relationships" between IDO and the United Nations.

The Soviet proposal, although not clear on all points, envisages a closer relationship between IDO and the United Nations, particularly the Security Council. The IDO Council would be obliged to notify the U.N. Security Council of any "infringements" by states of "their disarmament obligations" under the Treaty. It would be for the Security Council to take whatever "preventive or enforcement measures" were required for safeguarding international peace and security. Such a procedure would not be precluded under the U.S. proposal, which is silent on this point.

On the basis of information developed through IDO or on the basis of its own national intelligence, any IDO member would be free to bring a complaint to the Security Council claiming a "threat to" or "breach of" the peace under Chapter VII of the U.N. Charter.[18] The Council would be free to decide what action to take. Regardless of the relationship established between IDO and the United Nations under Stage I, the rights of members and the powers and functions of the Security Council under the Charter would not be affected.

The Soviet proposal calls for the IDO Council to "maintain constant contact" with the U.N. Security Council and to "periodically inform it of the progress achieved in the implementation of general and complete disarmament." The Soviet Union contemplates that the Security Council will have a substantial role in reviewing and supervising the activities of IDO. Close contact between the two councils and prompt, frequent reports to the Security Council are not in themselves exceptional. But it is of paramount importance that the verification procedures of IDO and the consequent findings of fact should not be subject to veto by any of the permanent Security Council members.

It should be noted that the Soviet position envisages that before the Treaty enters into force members would have concluded agreements with the Security Council making available armed forces, assistance, and facilities as provided for in Article 43 of the U.N. Charter. The United States has indicated that a U.N. Peace Force might well be organized along lines quite different from those set out in Chapter VII of the U.N. Charter. It does not call for the establishment of such a force until Stage II at which time the relationship between IDO and the U.N. Security Council would presumably need to be re-examined.

The problems likely to arise in IDO's relations with the U.N. General Assembly would not be so crucial as those of IDO and the Security Council. They would be more significant if the Assembly were called upon to act under the "Uniting for Peace" Resolution on a "threat to" or "breach of" the peace in connection with GCD.

Even after IDO was established, the General Assembly would continue to have authority under Article 11 of the U.N. Charter to consider "the principles governing disarmament and the regulation of armaments" and to make recommendations thereon to U.N. members or to the Security Council. If conflict should arise between the actions of the General Assembly and IDO, it should be remembered that the General Conference of IDO would be a relatively weak organ. Should those states not represented on the IDO Control Council consider the General Conference an ineffective medium for pressing their views, they might turn to the U.N. General Assembly where they wield considerable power.

Presumably, the General Assembly would be the organ to approve agreements between IDO and the United Nations. Those agreements would establish a series of links between the Assembly and IDO, including reciprocal rights of representation at meetings and of proposing agenda items. The Assembly would have the right to make recommendations to IDO. Past agreements have empowered the General Assembly to make recommendations on the administrative aspects of the budgets of the agencies within the U.N. system. It would, however, seem desirable for IDO to maintain complete autonomy over its own financing.

The International Court of Justice would be related to IDO in two ways under the U.S. proposal for Stage I. First, the organs of IDO would be authorized to request advisory opinions from the Court. Second, the Court could be asked to handle disputes over the interpretation or application of the treaty. The relationship between IDO and the Court takes on more significance at Stage II where the United States proposes that all parties to the Treaty accept the Court's compulsory jurisdiction,

101

a proposal which will undoubtedly run into strong Soviet opposition and a lukewarm reception from most Afro-Asian states.

The U.S. proposal calls for the maintenance of "close working arrangements" with the United Nations, and the Administrator is to consult with the U.N. Secretary-General "on matters of mutual concern." Presumably, he would become a member of the U.N. Administrative Consultative Committee which is composed of the chief administrative officers in the U.N. system. This body seeks to coordinate the policies and activities of the various agencies and prevent duplication of activities.

There should be few problems in establishing satisfactory relationships between IDO and the various specialized agencies for there would be little overlapping of activities. Arrangements would have to be made with these agencies to avoid duplication and ensure that any information supplied by them to IDO is timely and in usable form.

The relationship between IDO and the IAEA is a more complicated matter by reason of the latter's role in inspecting nuclear facilities, a role that would be considerably expanded if there were agreement on the U.S. proposal for a verified halt in the production of fissionable materials for weapons purposes or agreement on a nonproliferation treaty. Should such agreements be in force when IDO was established, it might be preferable for IDO to leave the tasks of verification to the IAEA, although eventually the functions of the IAEA would presumably be taken over by IDO.

There are other international organizations that carry out activities that would be of some relevance to IDO, including regional organization such as the Organization of American States, the Organization for African Unity, and the League of Arab States. Because of the reluctance of their members to give these bodies any real executive or independent role, they would probably not be appropriate instrumentalities for implementing a treaty on GCD. There are some functions they might usefully perform, such as working out agreements concerning the appropriate limits on the armaments and armed forces of their members and handling disputes that might arise among their members. In general, these states would not be directly involved in Stage I of GCD. On the other hand, it is possible that before that stage is reached various kinds of regional arms control agreements might be in force, such as the Treaty for a Latin American Nuclear Free Zone, signed in February 1967. Experience with these measures would be of value to IDO, and presumably these arrangements would eventually be integrated in the international framework.

Alliances such as NATO and the Warsaw Pact would be less relevant. Before IDO came into being, members of these alliances may have entered into arms control agreements which would provide IDO with experience and trained personnel in the field of international verification. The same would be true of such organizations as EURATOM, the European Nuclear Energy Agency, and the Western European Union, all of which have inspection systems.

Establishing IDO. Both the Soviet and U.S. proposals provide for a Preparatory Commission to be established immediately following the signing of the Treaty. This Commission would have a formidable task, particularly under the U.S. proposal, which stipulates that Stage I will "begin upon the entry into force of the Treaty." Establishing effective verification arrangements for the measures included in Stage I would require a considerable amount of advance planning, including perhaps agreement prescribing verification priorities. The situation would be easier under the Soviet proposal, which provides that Stage I would not begin until six months after the Treaty comes into force, "within which period" IDO would be established.

It would seem in the interests of the United States that the Preparatory Commission or the IDO Control Council be authorized to declare the effective date for the initiation of Stage I, such date to be dependent upon the establishment of verification arrangements. While this might mean some delay, it would clearly be to the disadvantage of the United States to have Stage I begin before IDO was in being and capable of carrying out its functions.

CONCLUSION

The task of reconciling U.S. and Soviet positions on the appropriate structure and powers of IDO is a formidable one, but the obstacles are not insurmountable. The resulting organization might be cumbersome but not necessarily unworkable. Even an organization that is "perfect" in theory will not work if large numbers of members or more important members are determined to be obstructive.

For the United States, the most important point should be to prevent any member from thwarting the gathering of information for accurate, reliable, and timely reporting, and for transmitting such information to the appropriate authorities. These functions are less likely to be obstructed if the system is adequately staffed and financed and if its operations can be carried out on a routine basis under centralized administrative direction. However, the verification procedures of IDO and the consequent findings of fact should not be subject to a veto in the control organ or the U.N. Security Council.

Without discounting the problems that may arise, one can conclude that it will be a more delicate task to get agreement among the major powers concerning the extent of the reductions to be carried out during Stage I of GCD and the extent of the verification machinery needed. It will be necessary to reconcile Soviet demands for substantial reductions, particularly in nuclear weapons delivery systems with the U.S. position that such reductions would violate the "agreed principle" that all disarmament measures should be "balanced so that at no stage of the implementation of the treaty could any State or group of States gain military advantage." Moreover, it will be necessary to satisfy the U.S. position that IDO must be able to verify not only that reductions are being carried out but that prohibitions and agreed limitations are being adhered to and also meet Soviet objections that the system favored by the United States would be so extensive and so intrusive as to amount to "legalized espionage."

In present circumstances, it may be possible to get agreement on only a number of limited, partial measures which would not seriously affect the strategic balance and would not require extensive or intrusive inspection. Various kinds of international arrangements could be established for verifying such measures, which might form the basis for the establishment of IDO if ever agreement were reached on Stage I.

II

DESIGNS FOR AN INTERNATIONAL
ARMS CONTROL ORGANIZATION

TYPES OF VERIFICATION SYSTEMS

During the negotiations on arms control and disarmament various methods for verifying compliance have been suggested. They can be categorized as verification through national external methods, or by reciprocal, mixed, or international systems. The choice of one method rather than another, or combinations of methods, would depend upon a number of factors, especially the nature of the measures to be verified and the number of nations participating.

External Verification

Under the external concept, each state might monitor the activities of other states by any means short of those requiring physical intrusion. For example, compliance with the limited test ban treaty might be verified by electronic reconnaissance, by seismic, acoustic and hydro-acoustic monitoring, by analysis of air samples, and other methods.

Many of the national entities created for external verification purposes have not been formal, but have been joint efforts or *ad hoc* committees created to coordinate the activities of various groups. Scientific activities such as seismic studies and intelligence activities such as electronic monitoring are conducted routinely whether or not verification is the objective. The purpose of external verification is to make the maximum use of data available, devise means of acquiring other data necessary for the particular verification task involved, and ensure that all of the data are reported to a centralized authority where it can be collated, reviewed, and analyzed.

Such external mechanisms involve highly sensitive intelligence activities. To reduce as much as possible the number of people and organizations involved and to prevent duplication of effort, the usual and most practical solution has been to establish inter-agency committees to coordinate the activities of the groups and their findings. These committees have the functions of gathering and evaluating data and of determining whether a violation has occurred. Since they report to policy levels of government, they do not have the function of determining responses to violations.

Separate organizations have not been created solely for the purpose of external verification. The head of one of the principal groups involved in data collection is normally appointed as an executive agent for the administration and technical supervision of the joint effort. Each participating group receives its logistical support from its parent organization.

In part, the nature of external verification is dictated by the sensitive sources from which much of the information is derived and by the classified analysis methods used. The tendency in such situations is to function within the intelligence community.

As progress is made in increasing the efficiency of instruments and systems for the detection and identification of seismic events, it is perhaps possible that verification of a comprehensive test ban treaty might be achieved by using such a detection system openly and externally. Such an operation would serve the needs of the general public for seismic information as well as supply verification data. Future developments of large aperture seismic arrays (LASA) field might have an important bearing on the practicality of creating an "open" organization for external verification of a ban on underground nuclear weapons tests. The effectiveness of external verification depends upon the degree of access required to verify the particular event. External verification is effective in monitoring the Limited Test Ban Treaty, but it would be less effective in providing verification of a cutoff of fissionable materials for weapons purposes or an agreement to halt arms production—two measures which require on-site inspection.

Regardless of the degree of assurance which might be provided by a particular verification instrumentality, no state could be expected to scrap whatever unilateral means it possesses. Much information gathered unilaterally would be based on external verification. The reciprocal sys-

108

tem envisioned for the freeze of strategic nuclear delivery vehicles would require an external effort of some magnitude to provide assurance that no significant changes in the characteristics of vehicles were being developed or tested. This function would obviously be carried out by participants who were relying largely upon unilateral sources.

Within any type of verification organization, the elements engaged in external verification would be designed according to the task assignments and the prescribed method of reporting. Differences in tasks would require differences in the background and education of those staffing the organizations, but their assignments would be similar in that they would not engage in on-site inspection. It is possible, however, that they would be assigned to serve in countries other than their own in those cases where it was feasible and desirable to conduct operations in an area adjacent to the country being monitored or in an area better suited geographically for monitoring by some technical means.

Reciprocal Systems (Bilateral and Multilateral)

The reciprocal system is one in which a state (or group of participating states) inspects another state (or group). In its simplest form, where the task is carried out by a party other than the party whose facility is being inspected, it requires little by way of international organization. On the national level it requires teams of skilled technicians who would be assigned to the inspected nation to observe and inspect facilities and events affected by the particular agreement.

Reciprocal organizations would receive most of their support from their own governments. Some support, such as transportation and communications assistance, might come from the government of the country being inspected. In most cases, the teams would be small.

The simplest form of reciprocal organization, an inspecting team from one state, would be feasible for such proposals as the freeze or the cutoff as long as the number of states participating was small. As the number of participating teams increased, a point would be reached where it was no longer feasible to employ a bilateral reciprocal system.

There are three variations of the multilateral reciprocal system which tend to reduce the number of teams without diminishing the number of participating states. These involve "pooling," which could be on the basis of formal or informal working arrangements.

The first alternative calls for the creation of consolidated inspecting teams from each side to which each state would be entitled to provide a representative. Under this arrangement, there would be one team conducting a particular inspection, but it would be composed of all interested adversaries of the state being inspected. Although it would be desirable to keep down the number of independent teams in a particular state at any one time, language, logistics, and administrative problems would have to be resolved.

The second alternative within the multilateral reciprocal concept involves a "pooling" of functions. It would call for agreement as to who should inspect such items as production facilities and who should inspect missile and space firings, etc. The data would be available to all members of that side, but certain members would tend to become specialists in a particular type of inspection. Although this alternative would reduce the number of independent teams in the field, it might require too much in the way of advance negotiations and agreements to be feasible at the outset. It would require such complete confidence in the ability of others to carry out their duties and such a high degree of data integration that it might not be practical without changed conditions and adequate preparations. However, it does have merit as a worthwhile experiment leading to eventual specialization within a future international organization.

The third alternative requires a certain amount of "pairing off" among the states on a geographic basis. Certain states would become responsible for the inspection of particular territories or states. Again, the data would be made available to all members of the other side. In addition to reducing the number of teams in the field, this alternative would reduce costs and would also tend to be a worthwhile experiment for careful study by those charged with creating any future international verification system.

Mixed Systems

The mixed system could be a reciprocal one with the addition of a small number of personnel from an international body. This is only one possible mixture of reciprocal and international elements. It is the evolutionary variant of the reciprocal system. Other variations in which the basic form is the international system with the reciprocal element as the additive are described in other sections of this study. The idea underlying a mixture of this type is to provide more credibility and acceptability to an essentially reciprocal verification system by the addition of an international, impartial element. Accusations and reports of violations would be accorded more credence if they were based on data supplied by international as well as reciprocal members of the team.

Several other advantages accrue to a mixed system. Such a system would provide training and experience that would be required of cadres used to staff future organizations, help to publicize verification in general and bring world opinion to bear on violations, increase the number of states involved, and give a sense of participation to more than just a few major military powers.

International Systems

International systems can be of various types. An international body might have responsibility for verification of a single measure of arms control or it may have responsibilities for a broad range of measures. The system might concern only a limited number of states or it might encompass the entire international community. The functions assigned to an international organization might be limited to the supplying of services or it might be entrusted with far-reaching authority.

International Verification System for a Specific Operation. This section outlines the differences between an international organization established to verify a number of measures of arms control and one responsible for a single specific measure, using the IAEA as a prototype for the latter.

The IAEA has developed a system for a specific operation: to assure that nuclear materials provided by the IAEA are utilized solely for non-military purposes and to safeguard other nuclear materials as agreed.

The great difference between the IAEA and other proposed arms control organizations is that the administration of safeguards against diversion of fissionable materials for weapons purposes is only one function of the IAEA. Most of the other differences are closely related to this fact. The same pattern might also prevail in the event separate bodies were established to verify other measures of arms control.

The IAEA seeks to cover all aspects of the development and use of the atom for peaceful purposes. The program includes research on the peaceful atom, assisting states in their programs by furnishing materials and providing equipment and advice, fostering the exchange of technical information, training of scientists and experts, and establishing standards for protection of health. IAEA's safeguard functions relate only to the program of furnishing nuclear materials to assist states, which is only one of the agency's numerous functions. Some nuclear materials furnished by the IAEA (e.g., radioactive isotopes) do not come under the safeguards program since there is no danger of diversion to weapons uses.

The existence of other functions, in addition to administering safeguards, has a number of effects on the IAEA. Perhaps the most significant of these is that the public image of the IAEA does not stem primarily from its verification functions. As a result, IAEA inspectors enjoy considerable prestige and popularity.

A second consideration is that the IAEA has been in a position to operate its safeguards system with a minimum number of inspectors and other personnel partly because of the availability of technically qualified personnel engaged in other IAEA activities. For example, four health and safety inspectors are qualified and authorized to carry on inspections to assure against diversion of fissionable materials. The Inspector General has the use of both the IAEA laboratory and Austrian research reactor. The IAEA training programs in Vienna are most helpful in developing the skills required for an effective system of inspection.

One of the great problems of any verification organization would be to keep abreast of technological developments. This problem is minimized where the organization, as in the case of the IAEA, has a broad program requiring knowledge of developments in its field. With such a program, it is easier to attract and retain qualified technical personnel.

The IAEA with responsibilities for verifying a single measure of arms control and with functions in its field beyond the safeguards function is limited to an area of arms control where the verification function is closely related to other functions. However, in an international situation where verification requirements are numerous, the existence of separate organizations of this kind would probably create more problems than it would solve.

International Verification System for Regional Arms Control. Proposals have frequently been made both to the ENDC and in the United Nations for the denuclearization of a specific region and for the limitation of arms in that region.[1] The Soviet Union and its allies have advocated a nuclear freeze and other arms limitations in Western and Eastern Germany, Czechoslovakia, and Poland. The question of arms control for a limited area presents a number of organizational problems different from those relating to the creation of a verification organization on a world wide basis.

One objective of regional arms control agreements has been stated to be isolation of a region from the arms race and conflict of the major powers.[2] The cases examined in this volume have one feature in common—the limitations directly affect the armaments of the great world powers. The great powers and particularly the nuclear powers have a vital interest in a reliable verification system since violations could materially affect their military potential and their relationships with each other.

The important proposals for isolation of a region from the major powers' arms race have dealt with regions where an organization exists with other functions which relate to the maintenance of international peace. These arrangements usually include provisions for collective peace-keeping and enforcement (a subject which falls outside this study, but which raises the question of the extent to which such regional organizations could be utilized to verify other agreements).

It would probably be feasible to utilize the NATO and Warsaw Pact organizations to verify an arms control agreement based upon reciprocal inspection in Central Europe. Both organizations have the technical skills to conduct a verification program and the objects of verification would be located in states adhering to one or another of the pacts.

The Organization of American States (OAS) has a potential for administering arms control agreements in Latin America. Its capability is enhanced by the membership of the United States which could furnish the required technical support. The OAS could be selected to administer an arms control treaty, although it is noteworthy that other arrangements largely outside the OAS were agreed to for administering the Latin American Nuclear Free Zone Treaty primarily because the United States is a nuclear power and a member of the OAS.

In the Middle East, the Arab League could not be utilized as the verification organization even if it developed the necessary technical capacity because of the existence of a state of war between Israel and some of the Arab states. Furthermore, the great powers are unlikely to allow self-inspection by either Israel or the Arab states. A reciprocal system in which Israel inspected the Arab states and vice versa is at present difficult to conceive.

It is also unlikely that the Organization for African Unity (OAU) will develop the technical capabilities in the near future to successfully administer an arms control agreement. Moreover, the membership of the organization is not coextensive with the region, e.g., South Africa, Rhodesia, and the Portuguese territories are not represented.

It is difficult to visualize a regional arms control agreement in the Far East because of political problems such as the opposition of Communist China to any arms control agreement, the division of Korea and Vietnam, and the tension between India and Pakistan.

Verification by regional organizations themselves is, however, only one of five possible methods for regional arms control agreements. The second is verification by a regional organization *under* the supervision of an international body. When the United States entered into agreements for cooperation in the field of atomic energy with EURATOM, the latter declined to accept verification by either the United States or the IAEA that the materials furnished by the United States were being utilized for non-weapons purposes. The EURATOM states set up their own machinery to verify their commitments to the United States. The United States accepted this method of verification on the understanding that frequent consultations concerning safeguards would take place, that the materials accountability system would be comparable to that of the United States, and that continuation of the cooperative program was "contingent upon the Community's establishing and maintaining an effective safeguards control system."[3]

This principle could readily be applied to any type of verification. The organization could delegate its tasks to the regional organization and utilize its supervisory powers to ensure the integrity of the system. It should be noted that this hybrid arrangement would have to be confined to situations where the regional organization had adequate technical qualifications. The regional organization should be permitted to inspect only the territory of its members. For example, the IAEA might supervise an Arab League system to ensure observation of a nuclear free zone agreement for the Arab states. A different arrangement would be required for Israel. It must be borne in mind, however, that the regional organization might not be willing to accept international supervision.

The third possible pattern for verifying regional arms control agreements is the extension of the functions of an existing verification organization. When the United Nations General Assembly recommended the study of proposals for denuclearization of Latin America, the U.N. Secretariat immediately investigated the possibility of using the IAEA. The chief obstacle to utilizing the IAEA in this manner stemmed from the fact that the existing safeguards organization was set up only to verify that the production of a specific facility was being utilized for non-weapons purposes only. It does not deal with the broader question of whether or not a state or area is producing nuclear weapons. This broader function necessarily involves the detection of clandestine facilities, a function which some consider is within the authority given to the IAEA under its Statute[4] but for which the IAEA has not yet developed the necessary machinery.

There seems to be no reason, however, why a body established to verify a specific type of arms control measure on a universal basis could not successfully verify a related measure limited to a region.

The fourth possible pattern is the establishment of a regional organization solely for the purpose of verification. In the absence of an international organization dealing with a number of measures of arms control or of another international organization such as the IAEA dealing with a related measure on a world wide basis, the obvious machinery for a regional commitment is a specific body set up to deal with the specific measure on a regional basis.[5]

The fifth possible pattern for verifying regional arms control agreements is the United Nations. As pointed out below, the U.N. has not been considered a suitable vehicle to verify arms control agreements.

Limited International Disarmament Organization (LIDO) for a Number of Partial-Measures Agreements. Under present American and Soviet policies of seeking agreement on partial measures of arms control and disarmament, it is quite possible that some or all of the proposals before the ENDC might come to fruition. If these separate agreements were to require machinery to verify compliance, the question arises whether each of the partial measures would require a separate organization or whether a single organization might not be established. From the standpoint of efficiency and economy as well as preventing too much proliferation, it would seem desirable to consider the creation of a limited international disarmament organization (LIDO) in connection with one or more partial measures of arms control, pending agreement on a first stage of GCD, which would require a broader, more comprehensive body.

International Disarmament Organization for the First Stage of GCD. The main difference between the verification systems for one or more partial measures of disarmament and the system for Stage I of GCD lies in the multiplicity of the arms control and disarmament measures to be carried out and in the kinds of functions to be vested in an IDO.

IDO would have extensive and diverse functions to perform, some in sensitive areas of national security especially for the major military powers. While verification systems for most limited arms control measures analyzed in the case studies are designed to freeze the military status quo in certain areas, the first stage of GCD would, in addition, require IDO to verify a series of reductions, limitations, and prohibitions, some of which are more difficult to verify and which would affect to a greater degree the military postures of the major powers.

The structure of any system for Stage I of GCD would have to be planned to provide the basis for verifying the even more drastic reductions and limitations called for in later stages of disarmament. Thus, states would require a higher degree of assurance that the system deterred and promptly detected violations than might be the case for limited arms control agreements.

Stage I of GCD would require an organization which would verify reductions in armaments and armed forces and take over the responsibility for verifying the limitations or prohibitions upon the production and testing of certain types of armaments. In the U.S. view, it would also be responsible for assuring that agreed limitations were not exceeded and that prohibited activities were not being conducted.

A verification system for the first stage of GCD would be costly and would require large numbers of highly qualified personnel in diverse fields. Its operations would achieve optimum effectiveness if they could be carried out on a routine basis with central administrative direction under guidelines established and supervised by a political organ in which the role of the major military powers would be greater than in existing international organizations. The agreement of those powers would be essential for the establishment and direction of the verification system, but not for its day-to-day operations. The system must be so organized

115

as to prevent any obstruction of the agreed processes for gathering information in the field and its accurate, reliable, and timely reporting and transmittal.

While flexibility is a great asset in any such system, in the case of a system for verifying GCD some flexibility would have to be sacrificed to the more important consideration of establishing agreed procedures and norms in order to narrow the range of controversial decisions that IDO would be required to make. Decisions to be taken by the administrator of the organization and the inspectors in the field would be more circumscribed than those of the control organ.

The fact that both the United States and the Soviet Union propose to vest the functions of verifying GCD in an IDO does not necessarily mean that all of the functions have to be carried out by personnel selected by, and solely responsible to, that body. In some areas that involve only the major military powers which they regard as particularly sensitive essentially reciprocal verification arrangements may be preferable. In other areas, these powers may require additional assurances that their interests are being protected through the appointment of their own observers or inspectors.

The need for large numbers of highly qualified and specialized personnel would make IDO largely dependent upon personnel made available to it by the major military powers. When the organization acquired a staff composed of nationals from many countries with the technical competence to verify a GCD agreement and when the major powers had confidence in this system, the dominant role of the major powers might decrease and IDO might have more characteristics of existing international organizations in other fields.

ORGANIZATIONAL PRINCIPLES
UNDERLYING VERIFICATION SYSTEMS

The organizational arrangements for any measure of arms control or disarmament would have to be specially tailored to assure that the agreement was being observed. Nonetheless, there are basic principles that appear to be generally applicable to the organization of any such system.

Factors Governing Size and Structure

The size and structure of any system for verifying an arms control or disarmament agreement would be determined by the functions to be performed and the techniques to be utilized. The factors that would govern both size and structure are closely interrelated, and this should be borne in mind in reaching decisions regarding the structuring of the system.

In a system in which each party relied solely on "external" means of verification, each would itself determine the size of the operation it wished to carry out. Problems regarding the appropriate size and structure of the system would arise at the point where an agreement required some kind of on-site inspection of facilities or activities.

With regard to facilities, the following questions would arise: What facilities would be covered by the agreement? How many would there be and where located? Would the inspection be continuous or periodic? If the latter, with what frequency would inspections take place, or if on a "spot-check" basis, under what kind of quota system? Would the agreement cover both declared facilities and possible clandestine operations?

With regard to activities either prohibited or otherwise regulated by the terms of the agreement, the same factors would be involved. It should be noted that some activities, such as missile firings and space shots, could be scheduled, but other events could not be predicted, as for example on-site inspections of possible underground nuclear tests. To inspect the latter kinds of activities, more personnel would be required.

The size of these operations would depend in large part upon the degree of precision in the verification process that the parties consider necessary, which would be influenced by the extent to which other means of verification were available and the parties considered them reliable. Moreover, "credibility" might be as important as reliability. If the parties insisted that the verification system produced internationally acceptable evidence, a larger and more internationally oriented system would be required.

There are numerous factors that could limit the size of the verification system. A system technically feasible could be financially prohibitive. The most significant limitations would relate to the degree of intrusiveness the parties would be willing to accept. The number and size of the inspection teams might be stipulated in the agreement. The acceptability of limitations on the number and size of the teams would have to be considered in the light of the freedom of movement and degree of access accorded to those teams. The size of the operation would also be influenced by the kinds of equipment it would use. The employment of sensors, for example, could modify the manpower requirements and the degree of intrusion. On the other hand, the operation and maintenance of complex equipment would itself require specialized personnel.

The magnitude of the verification operation would be greatly affected by logistic and communications requirements. Rapid and reliable communications would be desirable in all instances, but would take on additional significance in cases involving measures to guard against surprise attack. The size of the inspection organization would vary in proportion to the degree to which it could without jeopardizing its effectiveness rely upon the host country, other members, or other organizations to provide various services, such as maintenance of equipment, transport, and communications facilities. While the size of such an organization would be largely determined by its on-site inspection functions, it would be influenced by other functions it was expected to perform, including processing, distribution, and storage of data; evaluation of the information derived from the verification system; the need for training programs to ensure the availability of qualified personnel; the desirability of a research and development program, etc.

The two most important factors with regard to structure would be the number of parties involved and the extent to which the system might impinge upon national security interests, especially of the major military powers. A system that relied on "external" means of verification, or an agreement involving only a few parties and calling for purely reciprocal inspection, would need little by way of a formal organization. An agreement involving only a few parties might require only a means for consultation and a small administrative staff. The need to formalize the organizational arrangements would become greater when an international element was included in the system.

It is the major military powers that would be most affected by any arms control or disarmament agreement (with the possible exception of an agreement of a limited, regional character), and it is their interests that would determine the structure of such an organization.

The organization might provide for a plenary organ in which all parties would be represented, a smaller executive council on which the major powers would be permanently represented, a chief Administrator acceptable to these parties, and an international secretariat drawn from the various interest groups in the organization. In all probability the power to take decisions concerning the operation of the system would be vested in the Council to a greater degree than is usual in an international organization, and the major military powers would have greater control over the functioning of the Council than is customary. This would include greater control over the method by which the composition of the Council is determined.

The powers of the General Conference would be determined by the necessity or desirability of giving parties not represented on the Council a voice in the operations of the organization. An agreement might, for example, have many parties, yet only a few might be intimately involved with the verification system. It is unlikely that the plenary organ would be authorized to do more than discuss matters pertaining to the treaty and give its approval to decisions taken by the Council.

The functions assigned to the Administrator and to the staff would probably be of a routine character. The areas in which they would be required or permitted to exercise discretion would be narrowly limited, especially in any area considered sensitive by the major military powers. They would not be likely to entrust any significant functions to an international staff unless they had control over it or great confidence in its capabilities and impartiality.

In short, the interests of the major military powers would require that the operating procedures for such a system be spelled out in considerable detail. Subsequently, any significant decisions that needed to be taken would be made by the Council, and insofar as they involved the vital interests of the major military powers would require their unanimous consent.

One further factor that could have an important influence on the organization of a verification system is the possibility that it might at some future time be utilized for verifying additional measures of arms control or disarmament. If it were anticipated that the functions of the organization might be expanded (or significantly changed for technological or political reasons), this would have to be taken into account at the time the system was established.

Staffing

The major advantage of a reciprocal verification system, as has already been pointed out, is that each party (or each side) is solely responsible for the number, selection, quality, and direction of the personnel required to operate the system and, in turn, the personnel are responsible only to their own governments. The parties can have full confidence in the competence and integrity of the personnel operating such a system, a degree of confidence not likely to be attained in any other.

Were a limited international organization established to do no more than provide common services in connection with the verification by external or reciprocal means of one or more measures of arms control or disarmament, there would be no need to depart from the staffing practices generally followed by organizations now within the U.N. system. While these practices have not been completely satisfactory in a number of respects, they should be acceptable for an organization in which the staff would be small and would have only limited, routine functions to perform. On the other hand, an organization of such a limited character might have difficulties in recruiting its staff and might, therefore, be dependent upon its members to make personnel available to it.

If the staff of an international organization is expected to perform more significant functions, such as providing international observers or evaluating rather than merely collecting and distributing data, departure from the usual practices of international organizations would be necessary. If the organization were responsible for carrying out inspections, special staffing arrangements would have to be made, especially if those inspections involved matters that affected the security interests of the major military powers. In particular, those powers would seek a greater voice in the selection and direction of the staff than is the case in existing international bodies.

Direction of the Staff. While Western proposals have invariably provided for a chief administrative officer, the Soviet proposal for an international disarmament organization for GCD makes no mention of a chief officer and implies that many of the functions usually assigned to such an officer would be carried out by the Control Council itself, i.e., recruiting the staff, preparing the budget, etc. It would be unwise for the Western powers to agree to such a cumbersome method of operation. For the Council itself to decide on all details for administering the organization would be time consuming and would afford opportunities for obstructing operations.

To obtain Soviet agreement to the appointment of a single chief executive officer, it would probably be necessary to permit each major military power a veto over the appointment. It might also be necessary to provide a method for removing the chief officer for cause; to stipulate his term of office in the agreement; and to assure the Soviet Union that one of its citizens would be included in the top echelon of the staff, possibly by including formal provisions for the appointment of deputy administrators. The Soviet Union would be unlikely to agree to the appointment of a single chief executive officer unless it was clear that he would act under the direct supervision of the Council, would carry out its policies and directives, and would be responsible only for administrative and housekeeping matters.

Broader functions for a chief administrative officer would be preferable from the point of view of the Western powers, although they would probably not favor granting as broad a mandate as that given to the United Nations Secretary-General. These powers would no doubt prefer more flexible arrangements for selecting the chief officer and some provision to guard against the possibility that disagreements among the major powers might leave the organization without an administrative head. However, as the United States and the United Kingdom recognized during the negotiations on a test ban organization, concessions can be made on these points, if necessary, to obtain Soviet agreement to the appointment of a single Administrator.

Criteria for Staff Selection. The statutes of organizations within the U.N. system generally stipulate that the "paramount consideration" in staff recruitment "shall be to secure employees of the highest standards of efficiency, competence, and integrity." The second consideration usually stated is that the staff should be recruited on "as wide a geographical basis as possible."

The first consideration would be especially relevant for any arms control or disarmament organization. As for the second, the method of recruitment should ensure that the interest of all members is fairly represented, but avoid a rigid formula for geographic distribution that would complicate the problem of obtaining and retaining the best qualified staff.

Arms control or disarmament organizations would require a high proportion of highly qualified and specialized personnel. The countries from which these specialists could be recruited are relatively few in number. The more extensive and sensitive the functions that the organization would perform, and the greater the need for specialized personnel, the more the organization would be dependent upon the major military powers to provide personnel. Nonetheless, the attempt should be made to recruit on a broad basis, for an organization predominatly composed of the nationals of a few powers would be unsuitable for carrying out operations which affected a large number of states.[1]

Recruitment policies should be sufficiently flexible to permit the organization to obtain the best available personnel. An inflexible system implying that a member had a right to have its nationals fill a particular post, or number of posts, should be avoided. This might not be easy to accomplish, for many states are firm supporters of the "quota" system. The Soviet Union would be likely to require formal assurances that the staff of any arms control or disarmament organization would not be "Western dominated." In any arms control or disarmament organization, the desire to staff the organization on the objective basis of the highest standards of efficiency and competence would have to be sacrificed to some extent in order to accommodate the political and security interests of its members.

Recruitment. Responsibility for the recruitment, as well as for the organization and direction, of the staff of an international organization is generally assigned to the chief executive officer, functioning under rules and regulations established by, or approved by, the political organ of the organization. In any arms control or disarmament organization, the Council would be likely to exercise greater control over these matters than usual.

It would be inappropriate for the Council itself to recruit staff as the Soviet Union has proposed in connection with IDO. The chief executive officer, however, could be required to consult with it regarding appointments to important posts. In some instances, such appointments might be subject to the Council's approval, as is provided for in connection with the appointment of IAEA inspectors. It would be undesirable to make appointments subject to a general right of veto by the major powers, but they would undoubtedly have to agree with respect to the chief executive officer and his chief assistants. However, any party should have the right to be consulted with respect to any inspectors or observers to be dispatched to its territory, and specific consent might be required in connection with the dispatch of international inspectors or observers, as in the case of IAEA inspectors.

The Soviet proposal for IDO calls for the staff to be recruited from persons "nominated" by governments, and the United States-United Kingdom proposals for a test ban organization have specified that personnel be "recommended by, or acceptable to" the governments of which they are nationals. A formal provision permitting a government to veto the appointment of its own nationals would, in effect, recognize general practice with regard to filling important posts. This right should not be interpreted to permit a government to interfere in favor of the promotion of its nationals, their designation to specific posts, or their dismissal in the event they were out of favor with the régime in power. Moreover, the right of the chief executive officer to reject governmental nominees should be protected.

Many states are willing to make high calibre personnel available for service with an international organization for limited periods of time, usually for two-year terms. The Soviet Union has stated that all appointments above the clerical level should be made on this basis, and in practice, its nationals seldom serve for more than two years. The United States, on the other hand, has generally sought to protect the concept of a permanent, international career civil service. The practice of secondment of personnel has grown in recent years. Any body would probably have to rely on this practice if it required large numbers of highly specialized personnel to be stationed in hardship posts or to operate in a generally unfriendly atmosphere. In addition to unattractive conditions of work, the lack of career opportunities might make it difficult for the organization to recruit on a permanent career basis. This would be especially true if it had the sole function of verifying a limited arms control agreement.

There are a number of disadvantages to the practice of secondment, the most important being that it is sometimes difficult for a staff member intending to return to his own government's service to view the interests of the international organization as paramount. Often staff members leave the organization just at the point when they are beginning to make a contribution. These disadvantages can be mitigated somewhat by relatively long periods of service (at any rate longer than two years), by permitting seconded personnel to become permanent members of the staff (especially if they do not wish to return to their states), and by a well-developed training program.

Conditions of Employment. Regardless of the methods utilized for recruiting staff, the international organization would have to establish conditions of employment sufficiently attractive to secure and retain a high-calibre staff. This would include adequate provisions for salary, promotion, tenure, pensions, and other such benefits; in short, the same problems faced by any similar organization.

The problem of maintaining a high level of morale could be particularly significant in such an organization, especially with respect to inspectors who might be stationed in remote areas and whose presence might be viewed with suspicion or even hostility by those among whom they live and work. Boredom, unsatisfactory living conditions for the inspectors and their dependents, and even propaganda from indigenous sources could constitute a threat to the spirit of the organization. This threat could be met in part by efforts to provide the best possible conditions for living and working, including rotation policies which could mitigate a sense of isolation.

Of paramount importance would be the need to instill in each member of the staff a sense of purpose—a belief in the importance of the work and of his contribution to it. Constant awareness by those in positions of authority of the level of morale and repeated evidence of their support and recognition of the importance of the tasks being performed could go far to develop and maintain satisfactory morale.

International Civil Service. The problems of staffing an international arms control or disarmament agency on the basis of the concept of an international civil service would likely be greater than in those international organizations where such a high degree of competence and integrity of the staff would not be essential. Nonetheless, it would be in the interest of the United States to continue to favor this concept as a basis for staffing.

Under the concept of an international civil service, the members of the staff would be expected to consider the interests of the organization paramount and would be obligated not to seek or receive instructions from any external authority. The members of the organization would undertake to respect the international character of the staff and would agree not to seek to influence them in the discharge of their duties.

Some exceptions to these principles might be necessary. For example, a treaty might call for a "mixed" inspection team, where members of the international staff would be expected to serve under the leader of the team who would be selected by, and be responsible, not to the organization but to his own government. The basic concept of an international civil service could be compromised in this case unless the prohibition on instructions from any outside authority were specifically waived.

Privileges and Immunities. The basic principles governing privileges and immunities are generally understood and accepted. The application of these principles to this area raises some unique problems. The inspec-

124

tors (and observers) would require broader privileges and immunities than those usually accorded to diplomatic personnel and staff members of international bodies, especially with regard to rights of access and freedom of movement. Inspection teams might require a high degree of both emergency priority for their communications and immunity from arrest or detention.[2]

In a reciprocal system the rights of the inspectors would be spelled out in the agreement itself. Comprehensiveness and precision would be desirable, but compliance would be based not so much on legal obligations as on mutual interest in maintaining the agreement, the right of a party to abrogate the agreement, and other considerations.

A system involving an international organization would require agreement on the privileges and immunities of the organization itself, its staff members, and the personnel of governmental missions attached to it. This has been generally recognized in proposals that have been put forward. If an existing organization is to be utilized for verifying an agreement, revision of existing provisions for privileges and immunities might be required. If a new organization were created, the privileges and immunities could be set out in a separate convention, as was done in the case of the IAEA and the United Nations, or they could be annexed to the agreement. This method was agreed to by the Soviet Union, the United Kingdom, and the United States early in the negotiations on a test ban organization. The fact that this annex was agreed to with little difficulty,[3] that all three of the major powers are parties to the IAEA convention, and that both instruments recognize the special status of inspectors, indicates that agreement on the privileges and immunities required for effective operations might not present problems. This would be particularly true if, as has usually been anticipated in arms control negotiations, the agreement is implemented by domestic legislation.

In addition, a special agreement would be required between an international organization and the country in which its headquarters (and its regional offices) were located. If large numbers of its personnel were to be permanently stationed in any state, it might be necessary for the organization to conclude special agreements, as the United Nations has done with regard to its technical assistance missions and its peace-keeping forces.

While it is important that the privileges and immunities related to any verification arrangements be clearly stated in a formal agreement, it would be equally important that these privileges and immunities be protected against erosion. Should the states concerned and the international organization fail to do so, the effectiveness of the verification arrangements could be undermined.

Operational and Support Arrangements

One of the most difficult problems to confront a verification organization would be the decision as to what and when to inspect. This decision has two facets: (a) which objects of inspection should be chosen and the related factors of timing and frequency; and (b) the problem that arises when a host state contests the right of inspection.

Neither problem would present substantial issues when the inspection system was reciprocal. The limits on the right to inspect would presumably be elaborated in the treaty or in an agreement implementing the treaty. These limits might include both a ceiling and a floor on the number of inspections in order to avoid attaching any stigma of violation to the decision to inspect. Within these limits, the inspecting state or group of states would choose the objects and the timing and frequency of inspection on the basis of all available information. If the host state declined to permit the inspection, relying on the only ground for a refusal—that the inspection goes beyond the treaty authorization—the issue would be resolved through diplomatic or other channels. If the issue could not be resolved, presumably the treaty would have appropriate provisions for denunciation, or the parties might pursue various courses of action such as abrogating or suspending the treaty.

The problems under a mixed inspection system would be similar to those raised by reciprocal inspection when the mixed system involved a reciprocal organization with international observers. On the other hand, in a mixed system involving an international organization to which national observers or inspectors were attached, the problems would be similar to those raised by international inspection. The situation would become more complex where the primary responsibilities for verification rested with an international organization.

The number of occasions when the right to inspect would be questioned by the host state could be minimized by way of initial arrangements for access and freedom of movement, possible floors or ceilings on the number of inspections, and other points of possible conflict. Nevertheless it would not be possible in advance to foresee every situation and circumstance requiring inspection.

In an international system the execution of an agreement would be supervised by a Control Council. The agreement should, insofar as practical, relieve the Council of overseeing routine operations and provide the Administrator with as much authority as was politically acceptable to initiate and maintain data collection operations without continual reference to the Council. The chief of the inspection group in the territory to be inspected should be permitted to decide what and when to inspect (and also what not and when not to inspect), subject to the stipulations of the agreement, the regulations set forth by the Council, and the directions of the Administrator. The decision of the chief of the inspection group should be binding upon the host state in order to ensure the expeditious action required to maintain the integrity of the system.

If the host state challenges the authority of the international inspectors to conduct the inspection, a solution of the controversy could be sought informally by the Administrator and the representative of the host state. Should this method fail, the issue should be referred to the Control Council in all cases where, in the judgment of the Administrator, the inspection is deemed significant. The Council should be notified of any interference by the host country, since such an occurrence itself could be a vital piece of information, particularly in those situations involving anti-surprise attack measures. If the host state continues to resist the inspection, the authority of the Council to decide the issue and the nature of the response (action by the Council, recourse to the U.N., authorization of unilateral responses by states) would depend upon the kind of responses permitted under the agreement.

If the host state, without denying the authority of the inspection team, concluded that the inspections were unduly onerous or unjustified, a solution of the controversy could be sought informally by the Administrator and the representative of the host state. Should this method fail, the issue could be referred to the Council. This procedure should not stay or delay specific inspections, but would merely be directed toward developing new conditions governing the inspections.

Authority and Control. The paramount consideration in structuring organizations for inspection is to ensure the accurate, reliable, and timely reporting and transmittal of data. Executive authority and control[4] would be incidental when considered objectively and only a means to an end. Nevertheless, the means in many cases could be the key to realization of the desired goal of a verified arms control and disarmament agreement.

As a matter of principle, the effective application of full inspection capabilities would require unity of direction. Unity of direction would promote unity of effort by the coordinated action of all capabilities toward a common endeavor. While coordination would be attainable by cooperation, it would be best achieved by vesting a single head with the required authority.

The chief officer of any inspection organization at any level would operate under the authority and direction of a higher echelon or political body. For example, the head of a bilateral reciprocal organization would operate under the authority granted him by his government, since authority and control problems would be for the most part national in character and generally could be solved by the sponsoring state.

127

In a multilateral reciprocal system, unity of direction might be difficult to resolve because of the divergent interests among the states involved. If the relations among the parties in such organizations were friendly and cooperative, the solution of authority and control problems would be facilitated.

In a mixed system the elements of authority and control would require further flexibility. The exercise of the type of authority and control at all levels would vary in accordance with the structure, which would be tailored for the specific tasks to be carried out.

In a reciprocal organization augmented by international observers, the international observer is employed primarily to provide greater credence for and to check the credibility of the findings of the reciprocal inspectors. The head of the reciprocal organization should have the executive authority necessary to accomplish the mission of his organization and discharge his responsibilities. If, however, the head of a reciprocal organization were to exercise full executive authority over the international observers, the desired factor of impartiality would be under suspicion. .

Arrangements could be made to assign the head of a reciprocal organization the responsibility of coordinating specific functions or activities of international observers with the operations of the organization. Vested with such coordinating authority[5] he could require consultation between the organizations or elements involved but would not have the authority to compel agreement by the international observers.

In an international organization where national personnel were part of the inspection machinery, either as observers or inspectors, the elements of authority and control would change. The head of an international inspection unit would receive his authority from the Administrator of the international organization who in turn would very likely operate under the direction of an executive political organ such as a Control Council or Commission.

The role of the national elements would be: to provide assurance to their own governments that the inspections were being conducted effectively, to augment the international organization in order to permit it to carry out its mission, or a combination of both. In the first role, the most satisfactory arrangement would be to place national observers under the coordinating authority of the international element. In the second role, or combination of the first and second roles, it would be preferable for the national inspectors to be placed under the operational control[6] of the international organization.

In a completely international system, unity of direction could be achieved by vesting full executive authority in a single head. The character of direction, authority, and control would not need to be inflexible.

Any organization might exercise operational and administrative control[7] and coordinating authority and might provide logistic and administrative support for other organizations.

The organizational arrangements and the related lines of authority and control could be applied at any level of an inspection organization and would be particularly important at the inspection team level. Various mixtures of national and international elements could be devised to inspect different types of arms control and disarmament measures. Lines of authority and control could be established so that a team might be organized effectively to carry out its tasks.

In any case, nationals of a host country should not be given inspection assignments nor have control over any elements of an inspection organization in their own country. Such nationals might serve as liaison personnel, who would not be a part of the inspection organization and therefore would have no authority to intervene in the operations of an inspection team.

Data Collection and Processing. The provisions of each agreement would largely determine the methods of data collection and the structure to be established. The same verification techniques might apply to various arms control measures, and the information gathered to verify one arms control measure might be useful in determining compliance with another measure. Therefore, data should be collated to maximize the possibility of providing fully integrated information.

A unilateral or purely reciprocal verification system could collate data generated in connection with a verification effort, including national intelligence, to a greater degree than would be acceptable under mixed or international systems. In the latter type, it might not be in the best interest of a state to reveal all data collected unilaterally. The advantages of a reciprocal system in collecting data would be less if a high proportion of the essential data were provided through an international organization.

At the present time, the matter of on-site inspection is an inhibiting factor in negotiations with the Soviet Union. In the interest of reducing both the intrusion factor which might be disturbing to a host country, and unnecessary effort and costs, verification techniques in a host country should be kept to a minimum. The employment of inspection techniques which are especially irritating to a host country should be considered only when the information to be gained is absolutely necessary to verify compliance.

Regardless of the techniques employed, there is an important basic principle involved. The data reported must be timely, relevant, and in a ready-to-use format. The findings of an inspection team would be of little value unless the facts were available so that the appropriate elements and authorities might take necessary action.

A systematic arrangement would be needed to record items of information for study in an integrated manner. Such recording facilitates further processing and dissemination. It would also serve to provide a file on inspection operations and data for future examination. The importance of this function should not be minimized, for actions, interpretations, and procedures allegedly considered acceptable in the past might be used to justify subsequent action. Such allegations can often be confirmed or proven erroneous if good records are available.

After information has been collected, analyzed, and evaluated for pertinence and reliability, it would ordinarily be disseminated to the national sponsors of the inspection organization for interpretation. This dissemination would be in addition to the procedure of furnishing information to the Control Council of the organization. Since the national sponsors would have a vital interest in any response to a violation, it would be fitting that they interpret the information to determine its significance and its effect. The interpretation placed on each new item of information would usually affect previous conclusions in some way. Consequently, the interpretation process would be a continuous one, to confirm or refute existing conclusions. In any international verification system, it would be essential that an adequate volume of reassuring information flowed from one nation to another. Data acquired by agreed inspection techniques could be exchanged freely. Data acquired by national unilateral techniques would be disseminated among the interested states at the discretion of the acquiring state.

In the event a single international inspection organization were designated or structured to implement arms control and disarmament agreements, consideration might be given to having the Administrator of the organization, under the authority and direction of the Control Council, assume the following functions: establish policies, plans, and procedures for the data collection activities of the organization; coordinate activities, as appropriate, with outside organizations having related data collection functions to achieve maximum economy and efficiency in the conduct and management of the overall activities of the organization; originate requests for information where necessary (through or at the direction of the Control Council) from data collection resources outside the organization; develop policies and plans for data processing activities of the organization; develop and supervise an organization-wide program for the dissemination of data developed through the inspection system; develop and operate a data processing system and information center for the Control Council; and assign tasks to various organizational components in support of such plans and programs. The findings of a verification system would be of little value unless the facts were timely and available to those elements and authorities with responsibility to take appropriate action. All reports should be transmitted by the most direct channels to designated evaluation centers and appropriate head-quarters for processing and dissemination. Without jeopardizing efficient control and the necessary filtering of data, an inspection organization should include only a minimum number of evaluation centers and intermediate headquarters.

Freedom of Movement and Access Rights. Freedom of movement refers to the right of inspectors (or the mechanical techniques employed) to move (or be moved) from place to place without restriction. The right of access refers to the admittance of inspectors (and mechanical techniques) into a place not only to observe and record, but also to investigate and interrogate. Access rights might pertain, among other things, to ground inspection (by human and mechanical means) and surveillance by aerial and sea techniques.

This subject raises two broad problems: first, the method of obtaining the necessary agreements to permit freedom of movement and right of access; and second, the general principles governing agreements for freedom of movement and right of access.

Four methods for negotiating and obtaining agreements for freedom of movement and access have emerged from the international negotiations and practices since the Second World War. The first method is the inclusion of rights of access and freedom of movement in an underlying agreement or convention which calls for verification and inspection. An example is the Allied control machinery in Germany. The original agreements concerning that machinery, signed in the latter half of 1944 before the occupation, provided that "each Commander-in-Chief in his zone of occupation will have attached to him military, naval and air representatives" of the other Commanders-in-Chief "for liaison duties." In 1946 and 1947 the Soviet Union entered into agreement with the other occupying powers in Germany to implement this general standard by providing military liaison missions accredited to the respective Commanders-in-Chief of the zones of occupation in Germany. These agreements, which may be described figuratively as second echelon agreements, spell out the conditions of access, including the type of facilities to which access was granted and specific procedures for access. The agreements attempted to minimize the number and type of questions which would require interpretation.

The Soviet Union has advocated this type of access arrangement at various times during the disarmament negotiations. During the early negotiations for an organization to verify compliance with a comprehensive nuclear test ban, the United States and the United Kingdom proposed specific provisions regarding access and freedom of movement in order to meet the Soviet position on this point. A detailed agreement of this kind in the treaty would be less likely to break down under stress, since the usual pretext would be that the access requested was not within the terms of the agreement. Generally, states would hesitate to abrogate specific agreements. Even during the Cuban missile crisis, the military liaison missions continued to operate in East Germany and performed the valuable function of ascertaining there were no preparations in that area for military ventures.

The chief disadvantage of this method is that it is next to impossible to anticipate all problems which might arise over a period of years in verifying arms control.

The second method for obtaining freedom of movement and access rights is to establish general standards for verification in the agreement and to provide for a decision by the governing body of the organization on the extent of access and freedom of movement. This seems to be the formula which is contemplated in the U.S. "Outline of Basic Provisions for General and Complete Disarmament." Under that proposal, specific arrangements for verification would be set out in an annex to the treaty. However, the Control Council would be responsible for establishing standards for the operation of the verification arrangements.

This approach would permit introduction of flexible methods of verification and would not require a change in the basic agreement on the measures of arms control, with new ratifications every time technological or other developments modified the type of the required verification.

The third method is agreement between the disarmament organization and individual states on the extent of access and freedom of movement. The Control Council would then prescribe general standards for inspection. The details of access and freedom of movement would depend upon a specific agreement between the international organization and each of the signatories. This is the general procedure followed by the IAEA, but it is not entirely satisfactory. Despite the adoption by the IAEA of various resolutions on safeguards and the negotiation of a general agreement on privileges and immunities, the specific arrangements for access are not uniform for all areas.

There is some justification for differences in rights of access and freedom of movement in the IAEA system because of the three separate bases on which IAEA's inspection powers rest. But such justification disappears in the case of an arms control or disarmament measure when there would be only one basis for inspection applicable equally to all parties.

The fourth possible method is negotiation of the rights of access and freedom of movement for each individual inspection. Such a procedure is so ineffective that it would not be mentioned here were it not for the fact that the Soviet Union has occasionally advocated it in the past. The entire arms control agreement could be frustrated by the state to be inspected if it refused or delayed agreement on access.

If all parties permitted complete and unrestricted access within their respective borders, the operations of the inspection system would be greatly facilitated. It is doubtful, however, that such a *carte blanche* would be realistic. There is a question as to how far inspectors might be allowed to intrude into government operations, private industry, transportation and utility systems, research laboratories, and similar installations having a connection with armaments and military work. Intrusion which would uncover proprietary manufacturing techniques and processes would surely be resisted by manufacturers who wished to protect their trade secrets.

The degree of freedom of movement and access rights afforded to an inspection organization by host countries would be related to the prevailing international political environment, the intensity of their desire to reach an agreement, the desire to maintain a closed society, suspicion of foreigners, the degree of overzealous nationalism, and an insecure attitude toward their sovereignty.

While adequate freedom of movement and access rights might be granted by officials of a host country, a segment of the population might react unfavorably to such intrusion, unduly restricting the operations. These negative attitudes toward inspection might be modified by educational efforts by the host country and by appropriate legislation.

Problems might be minimized by establishing a relationship between the degree of freedom of movement and access rights on the one hand, and various categories of objects to be verified on the other. Full freedom of movement and access might be granted for specific areas and nonsensitive facilities. For other areas and facilities considered sensitive for mutually acceptable reasons, restrictions of varying degrees might be agreed upon. The ramifications and variations of such relationships are numerous and should be considered in the light of the particular arms control measure or agreement.

As a general principle, the capabilities and reliability of inspection techniques are directly related to the freedom of movement and access permitted by the country being inspected. Freedom of movement and access must be adequate for the accomplishment of the mission. Anything short of adequate should not be depended upon or tolerated in an agreement or in actual inspection operations. The object would be to deploy the inspection capabilities, including personnel, in such a manner as to provide them with the maximum advantage in their inspection effort and place the inspected state at a disadvantage in any endeavor to violate the provisions of the agreement. Freedom of movement and access require flexibility in organization, adequate communications, sound lines of authority and control, administrative and logistic support, and most important, the cooperation of the officials and people of a host country.

Communications. All levels of an inspection organization should enjoy effective communications. The proper operation of an inspection organization requires that the communications system be reliable, secure, flexible, and as rapid as necessary.

Most communications traffic could be handled by the facilities of the host country or by carrier, mail, or diplomatic pouch. Primary reliance should be placed on radio communications for traffic requiring rapid transmission or when other satisfactory communications means are lacking. The inspection organization should not place its operational effectiveness in jeopardy by relying solely upon the communications facilities of a host country.

As a matter of principle, an inspection organization should own, operate, and maintain its own radio communications network. As an alternative, it might be possible for an inspection organization to satisfy a great part of its radio communications requirements by using a reliable radio network such as that of the United Nations or by using diplomatic channels.

Logistics. The execution and success of assigned tasks and missions can be vitally affected by logistics. When considering organizational arrangements, however, it is not uncommon to dwell for the most part on the operational aspects and to a great degree overlook matters related to the necessary logistic support on the assumption that such problems will be self-solving.

The functions of logistics include the acquisition or provision of services; design and development, acquisition, storage, transportation, distribution, maintenance, reclamation and salvage, and disposition of materiel; acquisition or construction, maintenance, operation, and disposition of facilities; transportation, evacuation, and medical care of personnel; and collection, assessment and reporting of logistic data.

Logistics include both the logistic support provided by the organization and the intermeshing of significant elements, activities, or components of the systems or procedures of the inspection organization with those provided by governments or other international organizations.

The magnitude of the logistics effort will vary for each specific inspection organization and task. It is important not to base the development of principles and procedures concerning logistic matters on one type of organization, or one arms control and disarmament measure. The plans and organization of logistic systems should be simple, flexible, and practicable. Logistic systems and inspection operations must be coordinated, and the success of the inspection operations should be the goal of all logistic plans. Inspection personnel should be relieved of logistic burdens to the greatest extent possible.

Each organization should be responsible for providing or arranging for the support of its units with supplies and related services. In carrying out this responsibility, the Administrator of the organization might well consider the logistic resources and services which host countries, sponsoring countries, or other organizations and sources might provide. An inspection organization could receive logistic support from such sources when the support was operationally and politically acceptable and could satisfy all requirements promptly.

Financing Verification Organizations

The operations of an organization dealing with a substantial number of arms control measures would be the most costly ever undertaken by an international body. Even if some of the more expensive verification techniques (such as satellite observation) were carried out by states themselves, the manpower and materiel requirements of such an organization would still be formidable.

The major powers would be certain to insist on greater control over an international disarmament organization than over other international organizations. Their interest in effective verification would likely be greater than that of the smaller powers, who in turn would have less authority to influence decisions than they have in the United Nations. It is probable that many small powers would be reluctant to make contributions proportionate to the voice they might try to assert in the organization's activities. Moreover, the incentives for such states to contribute to international organizations usually would stem from the direct tangible benefits they would hope to gain.

No specific system or device, it is believed, would fully overcome these obstacles. No system would be likely to provide the necessary financial support for an effective verification system if either the United States or the Soviet Union held back their cooperation. Some suggestions which might limit the possible adverse financial effects of Soviet, U.S. or small power dissatisfaction with the system, are presented below.

Financing Reciprocal and Mixed Verification Systems. One advantage of a reciprocal system for verification of arms control measures is that the problem of financing is relatively minor. Within the limits set forth in the agreement, the state, or group of states, conducting the inspection determines the extent of the inspection that it requires and is willing to

135

support financially. The problem of financing the verification of arms control measures may therefore be mitigated by relying on reciprocal inspection systems wherever they are suitable.

The problem of financing should not be acute under a mixed verification system in which the international element added to the reciprocal would, in the main, consist of a staff to furnish administrative services to the reciprocal groups and impartial observers to serve on the inspecting teams. The funds required to finance this international element would be modest enough to permit allocation of costs through a system analogous to that used in the United Nations and other international organizations.

Financing International Verification Organization. It is improbable that an arms control organization would follow the procedures of the United Nations, where decisions on financial matters are left to the General Assembly. It would be more appropriate to adopt the procedures followed in the IAEA, where the organization's budget is considered first by the Board of Governors and then submitted by the Board to the General Conference, which may either approve or return it to the Board with recommendations.

As to the allocation of costs among the members of an international verification organization, the United Nations scale of assessments is used by many international organizations as a guide. This scale might be acceptable if the costs of the organization were modest and the functions it was to perform were of limited importance. It would prove unsatisfactory as costs increased or the organization were given more significant responsibilities.

Because of their limited influence in any such organization, the lack of immediate tangible benefits to them, and their general tendency to view arms control and disarmament as matters for which the major powers are primarily responsible, the smaller and poorer states would be likely to insist that the major powers provide an even larger proportion of financial support than they contribute to other kinds of international organizations. In these circumstances, the major powers might be unwilling to leave the decision as to the scale of assessment in the hands of a majority of the members. In the past the Soviet Union has proposed that the scale of contributions be specified in the treaty itself, but this would introduce undesirable inflexibility in the financial process.

The Soviet Union has favored arrangements that would in effect constitute a veto over the budget of an international verification organization. The United States might be willing to agree to this, despite the fact that any major power could sabotage the organization. In a number of international organizations the United States has feared, with some justification, that the smaller powers might exercise their voting strength to launch programs which the U.S. did not approve but for which it would bear the financial burden. It is not likely that this situation would arise in any arms control or disarmament organization. Rather the problem would more likely be the reluctance of smaller and poorer states to vote adequate budgets.

Voluntary Contributions. A number of United Nations activities have been financed through voluntary contributions when members have generally approved of an activity but have been unwilling to include the funds for its support within the regular U.N. budget. Examples are the United Nations Relief and Works Agency for Palestine Refugees in the Near East and the peace-keeping force operating in Cyprus. This would not be a satisfactory method for financing an organization to verify arms control measures since its functioning would depend entirely upon the willingness of states to continue their voluntary financial support. Voluntary contributions of money or equipment should not, however, be precluded, and might be the best means for meeting the initial costs of installing a verification system in cases where expensive equipment might be needed.

In at least two instances the financing of United Nations peace-keeping and peace-observation activities was provided by the states primarily involved—Yemen and West Irian. This type of arrangement, while suitable for missions to carry out a specific function of short duration, would be unsatisfactory in the fields of arms control where verification would continue indefinitely. Ordinarily, it would be in the interest of the state primarily involved to reduce inspection to a minimum. If states being inspected were required to bear the cost, their incentive to diminish the amount of inspection would increase.

Special Revenue Sources. Numerous suggestions have been made that the United Nations be assigned certain sources of revenue which would supplement the amounts received through regular budgetary procedures. Suggested sources have included utilization of the mineral resources, if any, of Antarctica, development of petroleum and natural gas under the oceans, and an international sales tax. Suggestions of this nature normally visualize a period of transition from the present United Nations system to a form of world government. While the later stages of GCD might require such a transition, it certainly will not commence during the first stage of GCD. Even within that time span, one may question whether governments would be willing to accept an international organization that was financially independent and therefore less subject to control by its members.

In some instances it might be feasible to develop a special source of revenue which would be directly related to the verification function. For example, in the event of a nuclear cutoff all future production of fissionable material would be devoted to non-weapons uses. The non-weapons uses which at present require the greatest production of fissionable materials are production of commercial power and water desalination. The cost of the accountability system for a power reactor is reflected in the rate which the power company charges the public for electricity and is only a small fraction of the total rate. Similarly, the cost of the accountability system for a chemical processing plant could be reflected in the plant's charges to its customers, which, in turn, could be included in the power rate structure.⁸ Under recent amendments to the Atomic Energy Law, this principle will be applied in working out the so-called toll enrichment charges made by the Oak Ridge, Tennessee, isotope separation plant for furnishing enriched uranium to the commercial power industry. The principles established for the electric power industry to defray the costs of safeguards are equally applicable to desalination. Thus, a part of the cost of verification of a cutoff could be factored into the charges to commercial customers receiving benefits from the peaceful atom.

Revenue obtained in this way could not cover the entire cost of verification. It would be neither desirable nor feasible to defray, in this manner, the cost of the verification machinery required to ensure against clandestine facilities, except to the extent that clandestine detection relied on the accountability system of declared facilities. Nor does it seem likely that the costs of the operations of IAEA headquarters could be met in this way. But by charging a substantial portion of the verification costs to the public in this manner, the remaining costs might be reduced to levels where there would be no problem in obtaining funds through the usual methods employed by international organizations.

Several objections can be advanced against defraying verification costs in this way. Atomic power is in competition with coal, oil, and gas. Any charges which raise the cost of atomic power would tend to delay its development and thus accelerate the exhaustion of fossil fuel resources. Also, the consumers of nuclear power would not be the only beneficiaries of international safeguards: the whole country and the entire world would gain.

Another field which may offer a similar opportunity for a special revenue source to defray a portion of the costs is the commercial use of outer space. It might be possible for tariff schedules for commercial uses of outer space to include some provision to defray the costs of an international system to monitor missile firings and space launchings and to verify that nuclear weapons tests are not taking place in outer space. Of course, the same points made above regarding the competitive position of the atomic power industry would apply to commercial organizations such as COMSAT.

Relation to the United Nations

In the early negotiations in the United Nations, proposals for disarmament or the regulation of armaments called for the establishment of control machinery "within the framework of the Security Council." Subsequent proposals have specified that the establishment of control machinery should be "within the framework of the United Nations"—a formula that permits a wider range of possible relationships. An existing U.N. organ or agency could be entrusted with the responsibility for verifying an arms control agreement; a new U.N. organ could be created; or a new body separate from but not linked to the United Nations could be established for the specific purpose of verifying one or more agreements.

The verification of the U.S. proposal for a cutoff in the production of fissionable materials for weapons purposes would be carried out (at least in its initial phases) by the IAEA, which already has established a relationship with the United Nations. Other U.S. proposals for arms control or disarmament agreements have called for verification arrangements separate from existing U.N. organs or agencies. While some relationship to the U.N. has been implied, the exact nature of that relationship has not been specified.

The reasons for the United Nations itself not being considered an appropriate agency for the verification of arms control or disarmament agreements, the possibilities of utilizing existing regional organizations for verifying such agreements, and the problems of coordinating or integrating the activities of a number of organizations that might be involved in such measures have been discussed elsewhere in this volume. There remains the question of the appropriate relationship between an arms control or disarmament organization and the United Nations, the organization which has been designated as primarily responsible for the maintenance of international peace and security.

An arms control agreement that is to be verified through national detection systems, such as the existing limited ban on nuclear testing, or one where verification rests upon reciprocal arrangements between the major powers, as proposed for the freeze on strategic nuclear delivery vehicles, would not require the establishment of any formal relationship to the United Nations. Of course, the agreement itself might specify that certain functions be performed by organs of the United Nations and that certain services might be furnished by that organization. Any such agreement could, for example, provide for reference to the

International Court of Justice (the U.N.'s judicial organ) or disputes over the interpretation or application of the agreement. The U.N. Security Council could be designated as the body to which notification of intention to withdraw from the agreement would be submitted. Both the United States and the Soviet Union have agreed that the draft treaty to halt the spread of nuclear weapons contain such a provision and also require that the notification include a statement of the "extraordinary events" which the party considers have jeopardized its interests and thus led it to withdraw. More importantly, the Security Council could be specifically designated to consider infractions of an arms control agreement, as the Soviet Union has proposed in connection with GCD.

In any event, the breakdown of an arms control or disarmament agreement would more than likely prompt one or more of the parties to invoke the political processes of the United Nations for an appropriate response. This would be true whether or not the agreement provided for the consideration of violations by the United Nations. The terms of the treaty could not derogate from the rights of any member of the United Nations to bring such a matter before either the Security Council or the General Assembly, nor could they affect the powers of those two organs as laid down in the U.N. Charter.

On the basis of past experience, and past proposals by both the United States and the Soviet Union, it is likely that any new international organization established to verify one or more arms control or disarmament measures would be largely autonomous, although linked to the United Nations in a manner similar to the relationship between the United Nations and the IAEA. It is possible that the United States might prefer a looser relationship, but if the organization were to include within its membership a substantial segment of the international community, it would be likely that a number of these states would seek to protect and enhance the position of the United Nations. In that organization, they exercise a degree of influence that would undoubtedly be denied them in any arms control organization.

The relationship between the United Nations and the IAEA is governed in the first instance by provisions in the IAEA Statute and second by the agreement concluded between the two organizations. If an agreement between the United Nations and any international arms control or disarmament organization were to follow the pattern of the IAEA agreement, it would provide for regular and special reports by the organization to the U.N. Security Council and General Assembly, reciprocal representation at meetings, reciprocal rights to propose agenda items, exchange of information and documents, coordination of various administrative arrangements, and consultations to ensure the most efficient utilization of facilities and services and to avoid duplication of activities. These consultations usually take place within the Administrative Committee on Coordination, which is composed of the U.N. Secretary-General and the chief administrative officers of the specialized agencies and the IAEA. They would provide the means for coordinating the activities of the arms control or disarmament organization with those of the other agencies within the U.N. system. Some agencies might be of assistance to an arms control or disarmament body, but it would probably be unnecessary for that organization to enter into any special agreements with them since there would be little overlapping of activities.

If the usual pattern of agreements with the United Nations were followed, any arms control or disarmament organization would be obligated to furnish the U.N. Security Council with information and assistance the latter might require in the exercise of its responsibilities for the maintenance of international peace and security. The agreement would probably stipulate that the organization consider any recommendations made to it by the General Assembly or the Security Council and report on whatever action is to be taken thereon. It might be authorized to request advisory opinions on legal issues from the International Court of Justice. While the Charter specifically authorizes the General Assembly to grant this right only to organs of the United Nations and the specialized agencies, the IAEA, which qualifies as neither, was given such an authorization. An IDO for GCD would no doubt be authorized to request opinions from the Court. There might be some opposition to according this right to an organization of more limited scope, but there would be nothing to preclude either the U.N. General Assembly or the Security Council from requesting opinions on behalf of such an organization.

In general, the relationship between an arms control or disarmament organization and the United Nations will be governed by whether the United Nations was expected to provide any facilities or services; whether the agreement entrusted specific functions to U.N. organs; and whether those organs, in the exercise of their own independent powers under the Charter, chose to consider and make recommendations on matters relating to the arms control or disarmament agreement. It is very possible, for example, that the U.N. General Assembly might be utilized as a forum by states opposed to, or dissatisfied with the operations of, a particular agreement. The likelihood of this happening would be greater if the arms control organization itself provided little opportunity for the members in general to voice their complaints.[9] This might be the case if all significant functions of such a body were vested in a

Control Council on which only a small proportion of members were represented, with the General Conference of all the parties meeting infrequently to carry out relatively minor functions.

There might be circumstances in which consideration and recommendations by the Security Council or the General Assembly on issues related to an arms control agreement would be beneficial, but insofar as possible any arms control or disarmament organization should be insulated from the parochial political preoccupations that dominate so many of the U.N.'s activities. Its operations should not be submitted to review by the organs of the United Nations in a manner permitting any disruption of the essential verification processes.

NATIONAL INTELLIGENCE
IN THE VERIFICATION PROCESS

An effective verification system has come to be, in the United States view, the heart of arms control. A foolproof inspection system, even if one could be devised, would be so costly and intrusive that it is questionable whether any major power, including the United States, would be willing to agree to such a system in the present or foreseeable future of the international political environment. We must expect that any inspection system will fall short in some respects. The supporting role of intelligence and its relationship to inspection become extremely important for a verification system adequate to protect U.S. national security interests.

One must distinguish the role of inspection from that of intelligence to appreciate the role of each in an overall verification system. Signatories to a treaty could find ways to evade the spirit and the letter of the instrument. Such evasions are the objects of an intelligence system proper rather than an inspection system. Inspectors are confined to the stipulations of the undertaking, whereas intelligence has an unrestricted and ubiquitous portfolio.

A signatory must be expected to interpret a treaty strictly when it is being inspected; not so when it is inspecting. The intelligence apparatus is not hampered by such restrictions. Its opportunities are at least as broad as its targets and its targets are broader than the treaty stipulations. The support given by the intelligence system entails the monitoring of all activities of the adversary to detect those which run counter to the letter and spirit of the treaty. The inspection system has capabilities to determine whether the adversary is complying with the arms control agreement. Since the inspection machinery is known to the adversary, he can determine what risks to take or what deceptions can be devised to get around the agreement. But the intelligence system, because of its methods of operation, has capabilities unknown to the adversary. It is here that the intelligence system serves to support and complement the information obtained through inspection. Where intelligence points to a suspected violation, the inspectors can focus their attention in such areas to determine whether there is a violation.

The inspection system should not be expected to ferret out the reasons or motives underlying evasions or violations by the adversary, and the fact of the evasion or violation will not necessarily indicate the motive. This is the function of intelligence. If the adversary violates the treaty, it is important to determine the reason in order that the other signatories can take appropriate action. The nature of the motive underlying the violation might lead a signatory to take no action whatever or to abrogate the treaty and rearm, not excluding sanctions.

Inspection aims directly at deterring violations, whereas intelligence deters indirectly by providing the information to guard against possible future violations. The inspection system is not a substitute for the intelligence system. Its role is but a small segment of the total threat picture. In contrast, an intelligence system is unrestricted in its task, operating to monitor all weapons systems—those under treaty restriction and those not under treaty restriction—as well as the military establishment and war potential of the adversary with the object of anticipating any form of aggression. It is the role of intelligence to monitor all activities in relationship to the agreement to determine whether the nation's objectives in entering into the agreement are being achieved.

Essentially, one main objective of intelligence is to provide timely warning of attack or of impending strategic imbalance. The time factor is essential to permit an appropriate response. The broader spectrum of intelligence with its greater range of activity and background information can, in some measure, make up for the inadequacies of inspection.

What then are some of the capabilities and limitations of intelligence in providing a supporting role to the system of verification?

Background Role of Intelligence

One may assume that much intelligence activity will have preceded any decision to sign an arms control treaty. The paramount concern of any state is the effect of the agreement as measured by the degree of national security it affords. There must be assurance at the highest decision-making level that the national security would be enhanced, or at the very least, that it would not be affected adversely. The source of data for such assurance emanates from national intelligence systems. By the time the negotiators have created a verification organization to cope with the requirements of the treaty objectives, the intelligence organization should have adapted its personnel, equipment, and methods to cope with much the same requirements.

Actually, little change is necessary in the intelligence activities of most developed nations in order for them to assume a role in verifying an arms control or disarmament agreement. The military and civilian intelligence agencies of the major powers have already developed the techniques and trained a nucleus of collectors and analysts for such arms control related functions as monitoring production, testing, and deployment of strategic weapons. An increased collection and processing effort might be required, but the product of this effort would continue to be followed by the same persons at the planning and policy-making levels as at present, with the possible addition of certain new officials at the national level who would become responsible for the various aspects of arms control. Some small changes in the types of data reported, the degree of detail, or in the method of reporting might be necessary. In general, intelligence requirements generated by those concerned with arms control would not differ from those generated by military commanders or national planners.

In most cases there would be no public disclosure of data derived from intelligence operations. The age-old requirements for protecting the source and degree of success or failure of particular techniques or sources would continue to be essential.

Certain overt sources of proven value to intelligence activities could provide useful data for verification organizations. Certain methods, developed and proven in intelligence operations, could also prove useful in verification efforts. There has already been some progress along these lines. The Geneva Conference of Experts in 1958 studied the means of detecting violations of a possible nuclear test suspension. The Technical Working Groups on the Detection and Identification of High Altitude Nuclear Explosions assessed the capabilities and limitations of possible techniques for the detection and identification of nuclear explosions at high altitudes above the earth and made recommendations concerning techniques and instrumentation. Additional studies were undertaken by Technical Working Group II on Seismic Problems with a view toward possible improvements in the techniques and instrumentation involved in the detection and identification of seismic events. These meetings and studies provided substantial information from scientists and other experts involved in related intelligence activities. It is in this background role that an intelligence system can be of considerable value to its counterpart inspection system without the danger of divulging sources or other trade secrets.

Active Role of Intelligence

An understanding of the capabilities and limitations of intelligence in the role of actively monitoring a treaty is essential. Three areas of weapons intelligence which are of direct concern to arms control and disarmament verification are: research, production, and deployment.

The research phase is of critical importance to proposals such as the freeze of characteristics of strategic nuclear delivery systems. The greatest single obstacle to intelligence collection in this area is the amount of lead-time required in the development of weapons systems. All such work takes place in secrecy. None of this work yields good intelligence indicators, because the planning, drafting, modelbuilding, computer analysis, tooling, and even the fabrication of full-sized prototypes can be conducted without much by way of externally observable signs.

The first opportunity that intelligence personnel are likely to have to detect the development of a new weapon is when it is readied for tests. By this time, several years may have elapsed since development began. The testing of all except strategic delivery systems and nuclear warheads may be conducted in remote and inaccessible areas and may go undetected in many instances. An intelligence-conscious nation may carefully schedule the testing of items such as new aircraft so as to diminish the opportunity for surveillance.

Similar evasive techniques do not apply as effectively to tests of missiles where the vehicle must be poised on the pad for some period of time prior to the launch. Since these areas can be protected from surveillance by aircraft, and by the provision of suitable surface-to-air missile defenses, there remains only the possibility of surveillance by satellites. Here, there is little likelihood of acquiring detailed information.

Another source of missile intelligence is radar. This method requires that the missile be at least in the testing stage of development. Radar also requires a more or less successful flight of the vehicle, since the vehicle must climb to an appreciable distance above the earth to be observed by radar facilities which are located in a state other than that in which the firings take place. Radar should be able to detect testing of penetration aids as well as other changes in configuration.

The material that intelligence personnel can normally hope to acquire on the interior workings of a missile is through telemetry. Telemetered data are transmitted to give those on the ground an indication of what is happening in the missile during flight. Since this information is transmitted by radio, it is capable of being intercepted by the radios of intelligence collectors as well as by the people who designed and launched the object. Although this is a potential source of valuable data, it also requires a successful flight and an understanding of the format used for the transmission of internal data pertaining to the missile.

The research and development phase of conventional weapons would be even more likely to escape the complete scrutiny of technical intelligence experts. Only through such sources as defectors or agents would much intelligence become available in this area. Often it is not until these weapons get into the hands of the troops and make their appearance in parades or maneuvers that their existence becomes known.

It is problematic whether any intelligence system that has not developed to the point of placing spies in the factories (not an easy task when personnel are carefully screened for sensitive production jobs) can provide fully reliable data with respect to numbers of weapons produced at particular facilities. Even were efforts limited to the production of strategic weapons, the task is extremely difficult in a highly industrialized nation where lack of information may lead the intelligence analyst to make too many assumptions for his conclusions to be reliable.

An understanding of production data depends to a great extent upon economic analysis which is invaluable in determining the capability to produce an object but is of little assistance in determining whether a decision to produce that object has been reached. Without a knowledge of what decisions are reached as to the relative priority of a particular item, the intelligence analyst working from economic data can only make assumptions.

In the case of such items as a ship or submarine hull or other large object which involves a unique manner of assembly and shipping, the chances are greater for accuracy of intelligence analysis than would be the case of such items as missile stages and components. The former require unusual launching facilities before they are fitted out for sea, whereas the latter may be built in various factories and shipped by rail, truck, or air to final destinations where they may be stored underground or otherwise hidden.

Fortunately, in the case of monitoring the proposed cutoff of production of fissionable material for weapons, the size and complexity of the major facilities involved make recognition feasible. Most undeclared facilities of this type would be detectable by intelligence. Nonetheless, intelligence would be hard pressed for accurate determinations of the amount of fissionable material produced in declared facilities or in undeclared facilities. Hence, the importance of on-site inspection of these and other production facilities.

The deployment of nuclear delivery vehicles, nuclear weapons, and troops with conventional weapons may tend to have different effects on a nation's security, and such deployment may be the very element that treaty provisions seek to limit or prohibit. At present, intelligence can perform its most effective role in the deployment phase. Even this capability will deteriorate as mobile launchers and ground handling equipment become more easily concealed or disguised.

A continuous program of aerial reconnaissance should be capable of detecting the construction of fixed missile sites. Locating hardened and concealed sites would be more difficult after they are emplaced. Aircraft capable of delivering strategic nuclear weapons might be visible to such reconnaissance as would large formations of troops employing conventional weapons. It is unlikely that nuclear weapons would be detected in this fashion unless special storage facilities and handling and transportation devices were observed. It must be borne in mind with respect to aerial and satellite reconnaissance that such factors as cloud cover and hours of darkness are likely to prevent these systems from approaching 100 percent reliability. Visual and photographic reconnaissance must usually be accompanied by other means of intelligence in order to make determinations as to whether or not naval units or large troop concentrations and assembly areas are merely associated with maneuvers, etc.

Technical intelligence collection in conjunction with observations in the areas of deployed weapons and the monitoring of broadcasts and publications can be most useful in the verification of arms control agreements once the weapons are deployed, but to provide detailed intelligence data concerning missile and aircraft deployment, some knowledge of the training being given to their crews is necessary. This might be most difficult to obtain when such training is considered to be sensitive by the state involved. Even if the type of training is known, one would have to know the level of training and the state of readiness achieved by the crews before the true nature of the threat could be properly evaluated.

Should intelligence be able to provide complete and reliable data concerning the transportation and deployment of the weapons and the degree of readiness of the deployed troops involved, there remains, in addition to the bugaboo of evaluating *intent* (always the most important but elusive factor in weapons intelligence), the critical item of detecting and monitoring the command and control structure of a nation's weapons management system. This aspect has the highest degree of security and must be dealt with on a marginal basis in terms of inference and indications.

The Role of Technology in The Verification Process

The role of detector technology in arms control verification is to improve the probability of detecting a violation and to make it possible to decrease the intrusion caused by the inspection and detection process. Both roles are important and can facilitate agreement on arms control with the Soviet Union. Increased probability of detection can result not only from better means of detection, but also from different ones. Unannounced introduction of a different means of verification (e.g., a new instrument) creates unpredictability in the system, which is an important deterrent to cheating.

To be effective, a verification system must have resourceful flexibility. Any single instrument or technique can be circumvented sooner or later. But simple changes in procedure can penetrate an elaborate camouflage designed to hide a violation. An inspectorate alert to the potentialities of detector technology can keep introducing new instruments, new procedures, and new methods of analysis, which—though of modest capability by themselves—can throw unexpected light into previously unmonitored dark corners.

With regard to monitoring a cutoff of the production of fissionable materials, for example, suppose the plutonium content of a sample is determined routinely by an instrument which measures the emission of alpha radiation. Other material which emits alpha rays could be substituted for some of the plutonium, and if the operation were carried out carefully, the instrument could not detect the substitution; thus, some plutonium could be diverted without detection. However, the substituted material resembles plutonium in only one respect: it emits alpha rays. If the plutonium content were evaluated by other techniques— chemical analysis, mass spectrometry, other spectrographic techniques, or any of a wide variety of methods unrelated to alpha emission—any of these techniques could be expected to unmask the substitution. Thus, the introduction of a different, not necessarily better, method of detection makes detectable what would otherwise be a foolproof means of diversion.

Another area in which technology plays an important role is that of data handling, data reduction, and data analysis and evaluation. In an increasing number of applications, sophisticated data handling permits the detection of variations which would not be possible by

149

scrutiny of the raw data. In the production and handling of fissionable materials, for example, the existence of large amounts of data, among which a detailed interrelationship must exist, facilitates the discovery of anomalies.

While technology can contribute to improving the verification process, mechanical devices can never be an adequate substitute for a flexible, knowledgeable, and imaginative approach of the inspectors. Fundamental to the type of inspection envisioned here is the concept of a small knowledgeable corps of inspectors probing deeply into selected and unpredictable samples of the system under inspection, looking for discrepancies in existing records, but not attempting to duplicate the entire accounting and reporting system. This is analogous to the technique of the United States Internal Revenue Service and the General Accounting Office. These agencies rely upon small numbers of persons to inspect in depth selected areas of existing records. Any inconsistency or anomaly in these records puts the burden of explanation on the organization being investigated. The probability of uncovering any deception by this procedure has proved to be quite high. The continued effectivenes of these agencies demonstrates that a purely probability approach to predicting successful evasion cannot be relied on where human ingenuity is a key factor.

There should be interaction among the organizations advancing pertinent technologies, the laboratories of the inspectorate, the headquarters and field administrative offices of the inspectorate, and the inspectors themselves. In fact, it is necessary, if one is to attract and retain qualified inspectors, that such interaction exist and that it cover the rotation of personnel among these different functions. Such interaction would help ensure that the latest technology is applied in the field and that the practical problems of the field are factored into evaluation of advancing technology.

The extent to which money and personnel should be committed to advancing technology is a highly arbitrary decision. It could amount to a considerable expenditure. For example, the cost of the single array of earthquake detection instruments, known as the Large Aperture Seismic Array (LASA) runs into millions of dollars. On the other hand, if the inspecting organization were required to accumulate seismic data on a scale beyond that now being done at existing seismological facilities, it would be appropriate for the organization to carry out this function in such a manner as to yield useful scientific data. This would have the advantage of making the entire organization's existence and expenditures more acceptable to the world and would facilitate the recruitment and retention of technically competent personnel.

With the rapid change in sensor detector technology, it is unlikely that any international organization would have sufficient financial or personnel resources to dominate the field technically. However, by acting as a focal point for defining the "customer's requirements," and by testing industrial equipment in the field, the inspectorate could be an effective catalyst to research and development and might make modest contributions of its own. It must be borne in mind, however, that resourcefulness and common sense in inspection is not likely to be superseded by advances in technology now foreseeable.

VERIFICATION AND THE HANDLING
OF VIOLATIONS

How violations of an arms control or disarmament agreement should be handled is beyond the scope of this study.[1] The close relationship between verification and response to violations, however, requires some consideration of the methods for dealing with breaches of the agreement insofar as this may affect the verification machinery, and especially the capabilities of an international verification organization to carry out its functions.

External and Reciprocal Systems

The relationship between verification and response to violations is likely to be less complicated where the parties themselves are solely responsible for verifying compliance, determining whether a violation has occurred, and deciding what response should be taken. The Treaty Banning Nuclear Weapon Tests in the Atmosphere, in Outer Space and Under Water is an example. Verification is by national systems using external methods of detection. In general each party has maximum

152

freedom in deciding what measures it wishes to take in the event of a violation. The test ban treaty does provide that a party may withdraw if "extraordinary events, related to the subject matter" of the treaty "have jeopardized the supreme interests of its country." A party might choose to denounce the treaty, in whole or in part, in response to a breach. It might also resort to an international organization such as the U.N. Security Council, but it is not required to do so. Were the parties obliged to proceed through an international organization, the national verification system would have the burden of producing evidence that was internationally credible to prove the violation and justify the response thereto.

The situation might be much the same under an arms control or disarmament agreement that relied upon a reciprocal system for verifying compliance. Within the limits set forth in the agreement, each side would carry out its own inspections, make its own determination as to the existence of a violation, and decide on the appropriate response. No international organizational arrangements would be necessary but it would probably be desirable to include in the agreement some procedures for dealing with breaches of the agreed arrangements concerning the operation of the inspection system. The Antarctic treaty, for example, provides for reciprocal rights of inspection of facilities and includes provisions for settling disputes over the interpretation and application of the treaty and for consultations among the parties on "matters of common interest."

International Verification Systems

If an international agency were established merely to collect and disseminate information supplied by the parties and to perform other limited functions (such as those described in the next chapter), there would be no need to provide for means of handling breaches of the agreement. The agency might serve as a forum for resolving differences but the parties would decide for themselves what responses they wished to make in the event of a breach.

The problem of the relationship between verification and the handling of violations arises in more acute form when an international organization is entrusted with substantial responsibilities for verifying compliance with the agreement, including the conduct of on-site inspections. The two principal questions that arise are: (1) what, if any, functions the organization should have in dealing with violations, and (2) how the structure of the organization would be affected by conferring upon it responsibilities in this connection.

The parties, especially the major military powers, might be reluctant to confer any such authority on the organization in order to maintain their freedom both to determine the existence of a violation and to choose their response. Possible breaches of the provisions on underground testing in the Limited Test Ban Treaty, for example, have been handled by the Soviet Union and the United States through relatively low-keyed diplomatic exchanges. If an international organization had determined the existence of the violation, it might have been more difficult to deal with the matter in this way. At the other extreme, the parties would hesitate to accept any procedures that would hinder them in responding immediately to a violation that might directly affect their vital interests.

On the other hand, an international organization would clearly be more effective in ensuring compliance with an arms control or disarmament agreement, if its verification functions were supplemented with some authority to deal with violations. Even if its authority were limited to determining the existence of a violation, this would be of importance in providing a firmer basis for the responses that parties might make individually or collectively, including an appeal to the United Nations.

As pointed out in the case study on Stage I of GCD, under the Soviet proposal the IDO Council must notify the U.N. Security Council of "any infringements" by states of "their disarmament obligations" under the treaty. Thus IDO would have the authority to determine a violation, although it is implied that the steps to remedy the breach would be taken by the Security Council. However, both the United States and Soviet proposals are open to the inference that the IDO Council would have limited powers to deal with possible breaches.

The Board of Governors of IAEA is also required to notify the U.N. Security Council and the General Assembly of any instances of noncompliance with agreements between the Agency and member states calling for the application of Agency safeguards. The Board itself has considerable authority in handling violations. It may curtail or suspend assistance being provided by the Agency or by another member, it may call for the return of materials and equipment made available to the recipient states, and may suspend any non-complying member.

Both the United States and the Soviet Union have fully supported the IAEA safeguards system but it should be noted that these arrangements apply only to agreements between the Agency and its members. It is open to question whether the Soviet Union would permit an international verification organization operating in its territory the same authority to deal with violations as that accorded to the IAEA.

On the basis of the past positions of the two powers, it would seem that they might agree to give the organization limited functions in dealing with breaches, especially those of a technical nature, but that agreement on the scope of those functions might be very difficult to reach.

Whatever authority the organization might have for dealing with possible violations would have to be vested in the Control Council of the organization, since even the determination of a violation would involve political as well as technical considerations. It would clearly be inappropriate for the inspectorate to have responsibilities in this connection. Since the Soviet Union denies the possibility of unbiased international civil servants, it would scarcely agree to permit nationals of other states to inspect Soviet facilities if they were to be involved in making such judgments.

Conclusions as to non-compliance with the terms of the arms control or disarmament agreement would be implicit in the inspector's reports. If these reports were to be used as a basis for action by the Council, it might make it more difficult for inspectors on the spot to secure the necessary cooperation. One means of protecting them might be to divorce them from responsibilities for investigating possible breaches, leaving the latter task to be performed through special inspections ordered by the Council. The Latin American Nuclear Free Zone Treaty incorporates a system of this type.

Granting the organization authority to deal with violations would not affect the size of the inspection machinery in the field or the kinds of powers the inspectors would need, but it might place a greater premium on obtaining technically well-qualified personnel and on maintaining the integrity of the inspection machinery. It might also require a larger pool of skilled personnel at headquarters, available for immediate dispatch to any area where a violation may have occurred.

To authorize the Control Council to deal with violations would greatly increase the desire of the major powers to maintain control over the organization. This could be reflected in the provisions concerning the functions of the Administrator, the composition of the Control Council, and most especially the voting procedures in the Council. It is likely that the Soviet Union would insist upon a right of veto over any decisions by the Council concerning the finding of a violation or the steps to be taken to remedy the breach.

The more limited and specific the area in which a major power veto is permitted, the greater the possibilities that the verification system will function effectively. Whatever benefits might be derived from authorizing the Council to deal with violations would be more than offset if this involved expanding the scope of the veto in such a way as to enhance the ability of one of the major powers to interfere with the process of verification. It would be better to exclude from the agreement any provision for dealing with violations if agreement on these provisions entailed concessions that might undermine the basic verification process.

One word might be said about the effect upon the verification system of including in the treaty explicit recognition of the right of a party to withdraw. There is such a provision in the Limited Test Ban Treaty. The proposed non-proliferation treaty contains a similar provision with an additional procedural requirement for notification to the Security Council of intention to withdraw. Neither of these two treaties requires the installation of a verification system in the territories of the nuclear powers.

The Soviet attitude toward withdrawal might be very different if the verification system were to operate in its territory. Throughout the disarmament negotiations, the Soviet Union has frequently alleged that the Western powers might not go through with disarmament measures once they had gained the advantage of having breached Soviet secrecy by the installation of a verification system on Soviet soil. The Soviet Union might be unwilling to allow an international disarmament body to determine the existence of a violation if such a finding were to be utilized to justify a state in withdrawing from the treaty.

Recognition of the right of withdrawal would have a certain unsettling effect upon an international verification system by calling into question its permanency. It would therefore be advantageous to include in the agreement procedures for dealing with violations so that the parties might have some recourse in the event of a violation other than taking the drastic step of withdrawal.

NUMBER OF VERIFICATION
ORGANIZATIONS

The "Outline of Basic Provisions of a Treaty on General and Complete Disarmament in a Peaceful World" submitted by the United States to the ENDC in 1962 provides for a single international disarmament organization responsible for verifying all commitments under the treaty. The Soviet "Treaty on General and Complete Disarmament Under Strict International Control" similarly provides for a body "to implement control over disarmament." If limitation of the arms race were achieved by agreement on a treaty leading to GCD, the problem of the number of verification organizations would not arise, since IDO would logically receive full authority and responsibility for all verification functions. If either a single agreement or a series of agreements covers several partial measures, the question arises whether a separate organization should be set up to verify each measure or whether a single organization should have responsibility for verifying all or several of the measures. Each alternative has advantages and disadvantages.

Whether or not there should be a single organization or several will depend in part on the type of inspection contemplated. If the inspection is based on reciprocal arrangements, the states carrying on the inspection will furnish the personnel, make the necessary financial arrangements, provide their own reporting channels, and reduce to a minimum the functions that might come within the purview of an international organization. If several measures utilizing reciprocal inspection were to be carried on simultaneously, a single organization might be useful to perform certain limited functions, such as furnishing neutral observers, arranging for communications channels, etc. The need for such an organization to take care of common problems arising from the several verification arrangements would be far greater if the inspection teams were operating on a worldwide basis.

The inspection of a freeze on strategic nuclear delivery vehicles would take place in the territories of the major nuclear powers or their allies, since no other states have such vehicles. The inspection system would probably be reciprocal. On the other hand, the verification of a cutoff would be worldwide even though a large share of the production for the next ten years would be in the territories of the nuclear powers. The system would probably be international with certain sensitive sectors being inspected on a reciprocal basis. On-site verification of underground testing would take place primarily in the territories of the major nuclear powers within the framework of a mixed verification system.

It is possible to include a limited amount of reciprocal inspection in an international framework. However, a single organization administering two different types of verification systems, such as those required for a cutoff and also for a freeze, would be dealing with arrangements where there would be little common ground. On the one hand, personnel for verifying a cutoff could be incorporated in an international organization, and on the other, personnel to verify a freeze would remain in the employ of the inspecting state. The international body would make arrangements to finance verification of a cutoff; the inspecting states would finance verification of a freeze. The international inspectors would report to headquarters data obtained in verifying the cutoff, and headquarters would turn over relevant information to other states. The inspectors of the freeze would, with minor exceptions, report solely to their sponsors.

While a single organization could have some useful functions even if all verification called for reciprocal inspection, the usefulness of a single organization would be greater if the inspection system is mixed or international and the area of inspection were virtually worldwide.

Types of Skills Required of a Verification Organization

The majority of personnel required to verify a cutoff would be inspectors or analysts and statisticians. Some inspectors would require a considerable knowledge of nuclear physics, nuclear chemistry, and nuclear engineering. A smaller number would require training in techniques of physical surveillance. The statisticians would collate and evaluate the materials in connection with the establishment of a worldwide system of nuclear accountability. Chemists would be required to test material samples, some of which would be analyzed through use of mass spectrometers. While undoubtedly some skills required for these technical functions, such as the ability to operate a computer, would be of use in the verification of other measures of arms control, the overlap would be slight. On the other hand, the techniques required to detect clandestine production of fissionable materials closely resemble those utilized in connection with other measures of arms control.

The chief skill required to verify both a freeze of strategic nuclear delivery vehicles and a reduction of other armaments would be a knowledge of weapons and weapon systems and their production. This would be fundamental both for verifying declared facilities and for determining the existence of clandestine facilities. The amount of logistic support required for the inspection teams dealing with these problems would be greater than that needed in connection with a cutoff.

Purely from the standpoint of maximum use of available skills, there would be considerable advantage in utilizing a single organization to verify a freeze on strategic nuclear delivery vehicles and a reduction of other armaments, but less advantage in assigning to the same body the verification functions involved in a cutoff or an unlimited test ban. Furthermore, there would be little or no advantage in using a single organization to verify both a cutoff and an unlimited test ban.

Use of Existing Organizations

There would be advantages in utilizing existing organizations for the purposes of verifying arms control or disarmament measures. The IAEA is, at present, the one international organization suitable for performing functions of this kind.

There are numerous reasons why the United Nations has not been considered a suitable agency for these purposes. Among these are: fear that the veto in the U.N. Security Council would obstruct the operations of the verification machinery, recognition that the U.N. General Assembly is too unwieldy a body to establish the guidelines and give the kind of supervision that an arms control agreement would require, the unsuitability of certain U.N. practices regarding financing and staffing, and the desire to insulate any arms control or disarmament organization, insofar as possible, from the kinds of political currents that seem inevitable in the United Nations. The overriding consideration is that the

159

major powers would insist upon greater control over an arms control or disarmament agency than they exercise over the United Nations.

It is conceivable that the United Nations might perform certain functions in connection with an arms control or disarmament agreement, especially with regard to the treatment of violations. The United Nations might also provide some services and assistance to organizations established to verify such agreements. But it is highly unlikely that the United Nations would itself be entrusted with the responsibility for verifying a major arms control or disarmament agreement.

The IAEA is actually performing verification functions analogous to those required to verify a cutoff. The success of a verification organization would depend in large part upon the gradual evolution of practical procedures which work and thus permit a high confidence factor. It would be unwise to abandon a satisfactory "going concern" merely to achieve a theoretically superior administrative pattern. The IAEA is likely to survive as a separate verification organization for a considerable time after the formation of an organization dealing with one or more partial measures of arms control, even if that organization could usefully perform services for the IAEA. This consideration should not inhibit the formation of such an organization or the establishment at an early date of appropriate relationships with the IAEA.

The factors so far discussed point to the desirability of maintaining separate organizations tailored to verify specific arms control measures. Other factors lead to a different conclusion.

Proliferation of Verification Organizations

It is possible to visualize separate organizations operating simultaneously to verify a freeze of nuclear delivery vehicles, a cutoff of production of fissionable materials, and a prohibition on underground nuclear tests. Three such verification organizations would rarely come into contact, and the total number of inspectors in any given country would probably be small. However, it is quite possible that there might be eight, nine, or ten partial measures of arms control, each with separate verification arrangements. This could produce a situation in which eight, nine, or ten separate groups of inspectors were wandering around in the states-parties to the agreements. The presence of a number of verification groups in a given state would be unduly burdensome and undesirable from the standpoint of efficiency and cost. At some point (certainly long before there are ten separate verification groups operating in any area), some consolidation, preferably through the establishment of a single verification organization, would obviously prove necessary. The form such a Limited International Disarmament Organization might take is outlined below.

Structure of a Limited International Disarmament Organization (LIDO)

The responsibilities of the verification agency would probably not be the same under all of the agreements. The functions to be performed would be spelled out in the agreements themselves, and they might call for different kinds of organizational arrangements. Not all of the parties to one agreement would necessarily be parties to other agreements, thus calling for different arrangements. For example, the financial arrangements appropriate for one agreement might not be suitable for another.

The structure of LIDO, accordingly, must be sufficiently flexible to cover a variety of different situations and to permit it to assume additional functions either under existing agreements or under new agreements that could be brought within its framework.

The General Conference. The structure of LIDO would depend in large measure upon the number of parties to agreements on partial measures and on the number of agreements placed under its jurisdiction. The parties might initially be limited to some or all of the NATO and Warsaw Pact powers. The partial measures might call only for reciprocal or mixed inspection. On the other hand, were the agreements on partial measures to include a larger number of states, an organization of a broader international character would be required.

For political and psychological reasons, it would be desirable to establish a General Conference, which would meet annually and in special sessions at the request of either a majority of members or the Control Council. This plenary organ would provide for participation by all the parties, whereas the Control Council would be limited in composition. If such a plenary body existed, it would be feasible to keep down the size of the Control Council and make it more effective. The General Conference would have limited functions of discussion. It would be empowered to consider matters of mutual interest pertaining to the partial measures agreements, including matters referred to it by the Council. Upon the recommendation of the Control Council, the General Conference would elect nonpermanent members of the Control Council, approve the appointment of the Administrator, and the budget of the organization as prepared by the Administrator. Approval by the Conference of amendments to LIDO and of accessions thereto would also be upon the recommendation of the Control Council. The decisive power in LIDO would rest with the Council and the functions of the General Conference would be principally to give its approval to the decisions taken by the former. Generally, the Conference would take its decisions by a simple majority vote, although on a few matters, such as amendments, provision for a two-thirds vote might be necessary.

The Control Council. The Control Council could initially serve as an organ of consultation. It would not be given the responsibility of passing judgment on the findings by the reciprocal inspection teams, which would go directly to the inspection teams' governments or, in the case of a pooled arrangement such as NATO, to a higher authority. Nor would it be empowered to determine whether such findings constitute a violation of the agreement. Passing judgment on the findings, determining the existence of a violation, and the response thereto would lie with the individual parties to the agreement. The inspecting parties and not the Control Council would have the right to decide what to do with inspection reports. By agreement the reports might be made available to the "other side" and to LIDO for circulation to the members.

To be an effective organ, the Control Council should be small in number and composed chiefly of the militarily significant parties. The Council would consist of two classes of membership—permanent and nonpermanent. The major military powers would be permanent members, while the nonpermanent members would be elected on a rotating basis. The number of nonpermanent members from the Soviet side and from the Western side would have to be fixed on a basis that took into consideration the greater number of states on the Western side and the insistence of the Soviet Union on "parity." Some provision would have to be made for the participation of other parties when matters which affect them were being considered.

While there has been increasing recognition in many international bodies of the desirability of avoiding formal votes insofar as possible, there will be occasions when voting will be necessary. To which decisions in the Control Council the principle of unanimity of the permanent members would apply should be clearly spelled out.[1] However, they should not extend to the day-to-day operations of LIDO.

In the event of disputes arising in connection with the implementation of the partial measures agreements, the Control Council would be the appropriate organ for settling them. Where the disputes relate to the interpretation or application of agreements and are not resolved by negotiations in the Control Council, provision should be made for resort to the International Court of Justice.

Administrator. Under LIDO, the Administrator would be chosen by the Control Council, and approved by the General Conference. He should be acceptable to the major interest groups, including the permanent members. While the experience of the United Nations argues against any "veto" over the selection of the chief executive of an international organization, a concession on this point might have to be made to the Soviet Union in order to obtain its agreement. As has been previously pointed out, this fact was recognized by both the United States and the United Kingdom during the test ban treaty negotiations when they conceded that the appointment of both the Administrator and the First Deputy Administrator would require the approval of the United States, the United Kingdom, and the Soviet Union.

The LIDO Administrator should be appointed for at least a three or four year term and should be eligible for reappointment. This term is of sufficient length to enable the Administrator to prove his worth and his continuing acceptability to the permanent members.

With LIDO limited in powers and functions and the reciprocal verification system in the hands of the signatories, the duties and functions of the Administrator would not be extensive. As the chief administrative officer, he would perform his duties in conformity with the regulations adopted by the Control Council. He would be responsible for the organization, selection, and functioning of the staff under the authority of and subject to the Control Council.

The Administrator might act as a depository of reports relating to inspections carried out by the inspecting parties and supply them with common services. He would provide the secretariat for the meetings of the Control Council and the General Conference, keep records and publish reports, and supply required documentation. The staff could be the source for international observer personnel to accompany the reciprocal inspectors on their tours of inspections, thus, in a way combining the characteristics of both the reciprocal and the impartial principles of verification. This mixed design would add greater credibility to the findings of the inspectors and give the system greater acceptability.

The Administrator might render his good offices in controversies relating to such matters as the permissibility of, and rights and duties with respect to, inspection, a function which need not be formally stated. Possible controversies such as these should be distinguished from disputes as to whether or not the facts disclosed by the inspectors should be adjudged to be a violation of the agreement. This function would be solely the responsibility of the aggrieved party or parties to the agreement.

LIDO would plan for the orderly administrative development of verification systems. The Administrator, subject to direction from the Control Council, would be entrusted with these responsibilities. The Control Council might empower the Administrator to perform other duties in connection with matters arising out of the verification system.

The Staff. LIDO should have a staff adequate to carry out effectively and impartially the tasks entrusted to it. Since it would have limited functions, the staff need not be large, especially in the initial stages. The United States has advocated the concept of an international civil service for international organizations. Presumably, it would favor staffing LIDO on a similar basis. The Soviet Union has stated in the past that an impartial international civil service is not attainable.

If LIDO is to supply international observers as the "mix" in the reciprocal inspection teams, the appointment of such personnel to the staff would need the approval of the Control Council and might require, in addition, the concurrence of the permanent members. The designation by the Administrator of a particular observer or observers to accompany a reciprocal inspection team might also require the consent of the member being inspected. The international observer should not be a national serving on a team inspecting his own state, nor a national of a reciprocal team doing the inspecting.

Inspection Teams. The international observers of LIDO would be attached to inspection teams on the request of one or both parties in a reciprocal system. While they might participate in the work of the team, their primary purpose would be to observe the work of the team and report to the Administrator. Their presence would lend credibility to the findings of the inspection and would also tend to discourage one side from denying the validity of the other's findings. The reports of international observers would be available to countries doing the inspecting, to those being inspected, as well as to other members of the organization.

Should LIDO at some stage be given responsibility for carrying out inspections, national observers, paid by their governments, might be attached to the international inspection teams. Their chief purpose would be to assure their governments that the inspections were being conducted effectively. They would function under the coordinating authority of LIDO, but they would be free to report directly to their governments without having such reports channeled through LIDO. Another possibility for the composition of a LIDO inspection team is the seconding of nationals to serve as inspectors. In this instance, the seconded nationals would serve as members of the LIDO staff and would be subject to the operational control of LIDO. They would report to their own governments only if permitted to do so under the agreement. The seconding principle can provide LIDO with specially needed skilled personnel. The national observers would not be a part of the LIDO staff but would be accorded the privileges and immunities necessary to carry out their functions.

Financial Questions. The operations of LIDO under a system with limited functions (where the cost of inspections is borne by the reciprocal parties) would not be a financial burden. Were it to provide the international observers in a mixed system, or empowered to carry out inspections, the cost would increase considerably. The budget for LIDO should be prepared by the Administrator, recommended by the Council, and approved by the Conference, as the United States has proposed.

Under LIDO, the political realities within the context of arms control and disarmament programs appear to call for placing the control of the budget in the hands of the Control Council, with the General Conference having the function of approving by a simple majority vote what the Control Council has recommended.

Expenditures of LIDO would be borne by the parties in accordance with a scale of apportionment approved by the Control Council. Such a scale, however, would have to be tailored to meet the nature of LIDO's responsibilities. Past experience in the U.N. on financing peace-keeping operations indicates that the smaller powers expect the larger states to bear a heavier share of the financial burden for extraordinary operations. It is likely this would also be the case with LIDO.

Access. The problem of access is crucial. Any role of LIDO in inspection would not arise until it was authorized to furnish observers to accompany reciprocal inspection teams. The access agreements for reciprocal inspection could include LIDO's participation in this capacity.

As LIDO's functions are enlarged, access agreements between LIDO and the parties might be required to enable LIDO to carry out the additional functions relating to inspections entrusted to it. The agreement for the partial measure should spell out with as much particularity as feasible the principles of access.

The extent of access inside the territory of a party to the agreement would be governed by the nature of the object to be inspected and the risk involved from possible violations. Witnessing the destruction of armaments at specific locations within a nation's territory, for example, would not involve a high degree of access, whereas inspection to discover undeclared sites in cases selected by the inspectorate would require considerable access.

Privileges and Immunities. The status of teams of the reciprocal type, be they resident or otherwise, could be no less than those of an inspectorate under an international organization. Presumably the partial arms control agreement would define their status along the same lines as that accorded IAEA inspectors and their staff, technical assistance missions, or United Nations peace-keeping missions.

The status of LIDO, the representatives attached to it, the headquarters staff, and the personnel that accompany a reciprocal inspection team, should cause no negotiating problems in view of well-established practices. These matters should be spelled out in the instrument setting up LIDO.

Amendments. The organic instruments of international organizations differ from most multilateral treaties in that a qualified majority of members may adopt amendments that are binding upon all members. Under the Charter of the United Nations, amendments come into force after they have been approved and ratified by two-thirds of the members of the organization, including all the permanent members of the Security Council.

Under the U.S. Outline of a Treaty for General and Complete Disarmament, the language with respect to amendments merely calls for agreement "to specific procedures for considering amendments or modifications . . . in the light of experience in the early period of implementation" of the treaty. Amendments would require approval by the General Conference. The Soviet Draft Treaty on General and Complete Disarmament is more specific. It requires that amendments be adopted by two-thirds of all the parties to the treaty and ratified by (a) all the permanent members of the U.N. Security Council; (b) those states that are "their allies in bilateral and multilateral military arrangements;" and (c) an unspecified number of other states. Since it is envisaged that LIDO would be an expanding organization, amendments to its organic instrument ought not be made difficult. Adoption and ratification of amendments by a simple majority should be the aim. Amendments should require the consent of the permanent members of the Control Council, since the operations of LIDO relate intimately to their security.

A procedural device by which the obligations of the parties might be changed without formal amendment, which might be particularly appropriate for LIDO, is suggested in the U.S. Outline of a Treaty on General and Complete Disarmament. A subsidiary organ of the Control Council would study "the codification and progressive development of rules of international conduct related to disarmament" and recommend "rules" for approval by the Control Council. The rules would become effective three months after adoption unless a majority of the parties signified their disapproval, and all parties would be bound by the rules unless they formally notified the international disarmament organization within a year that "they do not consider themselves so bound."

Relation to the United Nations and Other International Organizations. The most desirable relationship between LIDO and the United Nations would be that of an autonomous international organization within the United Nations system. Its relationship should be patterned after the IAEA, which reports directly to the General Assembly and the Security Council.

Regardless of the relationship established between LIDO and the United Nations, the rights of the signatories to resort to the Security Council in connection with the implementation of the agreement on arms control would not be impaired. Here the Security Council would be free to decide what, if any, action it would take, as would the General

Assembly were it called upon to act under the Uniting for Peace Resolution.

The relationship agreement between LIDO and the United Nations could, *inter alia*, provide for reciprocal rights of representation at meetings and authorize the Administrator to consult with the Secretary-General on matters of mutual concern and to attend meetings of the U.N. Administrative Consultative Committee, which is comprised of all the chief administrative officers in the U.N. system and seeks to coordinate the policies and activities of the various agencies. LIDO would submit to the United Nations annual reports on the activities of the organization. The General Assembly might authorize LIDO to request advisory opinions from the International Court of Justice. While past agreements have empowered the U.N. General Assembly to make recommendations on the administrative aspects of the budgets of the agencies within the system, it would be desirable for LIDO, in view of its special character, to maintain complete financial autonomy.

In the initial stage, with its role essentially as a service organization in connection with reciprocal inspection, LIDO would probably have no need to set up a relationship with such regional organizations as the Organization of American States, the Organization for African Unity, and the League of Arab States. By the time the scope and authority of LIDO was extended, various kinds of regional arms control agreements might well have come into being. Such arrangements could be absorbed within the framework of LIDO.

Time Factor. No single factor would determine whether there should be one or several verification organizations. Nor would the organizational pattern be static. The time factor would certainly be of maximum importance. If areas of accord develop slowly, a specific organization tailored to verify each measure would probably evolve. On the other hand, if the development of areas of accord were rapid, with several partial measures being agreed upon, there would be a greater tendency to set up a single organization with multiple functions.

It is difficult to devise a simple formula to determine whether a single body should have responsibility for verifying a group of partial arms control measures or whether separate bodies should verify each measure. A separate organization might be preferable where: the method of verification requires skills only remotely related to those required to verify other measures; the information derived from the verification process was of little relevance or importance to the verification of other measures; and the cost of the verification was relatively small.

On the other hand, a single organization to verify several partial measures would be preferable where: the several methods of verification utilized common services, the necessary skills were similar for the several methods of verification, the data derived from the verification of the several measures tended to be mutually self-supporting, and the costs were sufficiently great to require the most efficient use of financial resources. In the process of centralizing verification functions, however, great care should be taken to avoid destroying successful procedures and techniques. A "going concern" should not be sacrificed to theoretical organizational concepts.

NOTES

Introduction

1. ENDC/PV.164, February 6, 1964, p. 5.

2. *Ibid.,* p. 6.

3. See The New York *Times,* December 3, 1967, for the text of the President's statement.

4. *Ibid.*

5. U.S. Department of State *Bulletin,* November 2, 1963, pp. 610–614.

6. Mason Willrich, "Guarantees to Non-Nuclear Nations," *Foreign Affairs,* July, 1966, pp. 683–692.

7. See General Assembly Resolution 2028 (XX).

8. Document ENDC/C.1/1.

9. *Current History,* August 1964, pp. 107–108.

10. *The United Nations and Disarmament, 1945–1965* (United Nations, New York), p. 232.

11. ENDC/120.

12. ENDC/PV.162.

13. The ENDC is the successor to the Ten Nation Disarmament Committee which was composed of five members of the Warsaw Pact and five NATO members. The new committee includes eight additional states, none of which was a member of either pact. It is outside of, but linked to, the United Nations.

14. *Official Records of the Disarmament Commission,* Supplement for January 1961 to December 1962. Document DC/203.

PART I

ORGANIZATIONAL ARRANGEMENTS FOR VERIFYING ARMS CONTROL

Case 1

1. For an extended treatment of the Baruch Plan and successor proposals, see B. G. Bechhoefer, *Postwar Negotiations for Arms Control* (Washington, D.C.: The Brookings Institution, 1961).

2. In his speech to the United Nations General Assembly on December 8, 1953, President Eisenhower proposed a program of "Atoms for Peace." This proposal in due course led to the formal creation of the IAEA in 1957. The Statute of the IAEA sets up several types of safeguards responsibilities. For a detailed account of the Agency's safeguards system see John A. Hall's article, "The Safeguards Role of the International Atomic Energy Agency," *Disarmament and Arms Control,* Vol. II, No. 2 (1964), pp. 170–186.

3. D. Okrent, "Nuclear Considerations in the Selection of Materials for Fast Reactors," American Nuclear Society, AIME Symposium, November 1963. This paper does not consider problems which may arise from limiting the production of tritium, since the overall effect of such measures would not affect the conclusions materially.

4. R. P. Wischow, *et. al.*, "Safeguards Procedures for a Nuclear Fuel Reprocessing Plant," Argonne National Laboratory Symposium, June 1967.

5. *Ibid.*, pp 4–5.

6. *Ibid.*, p. 6.

7. ENDC/134, June 25, 1964, p. 3.

8. This point is not necessarily in conflict with the current United States proposal for perimeter control; see discussion below.

9. The *side feeds* come primarily from scrap and spent reactor fuel.

10. The *side withdrawals* are primarily for fueling slightly enriched reactors.

11. Hanford Atomic Products Operation Staff, *Reactor Shutdown Inspection System*, USAEC Report RL–REA–26, November 25, 1964; A. de la Garza and C. R. Milone, *Material Control and Inspection at a Gaseous Diffusion Plant*, USAEC Report KOA–611, 1959; F. S. Patton, *International Monitoring of a Very Highly Enriched Uranium Facility*, USAEC Report Y–1305, 1960.

12. Hanford Atomic Products Operation Staff, *Tamper-Indicating Safing System*, USAEC Report RL–REA–2228, July 12, 1965.

13. ENDC/134, June 25, 1964, p. 4.

14. For a fuller treatment of the IAEA, see B. G. Bechhoefer, "Negotiating the Statute of the International Atomic Energy Agency," *International Organization*, Vol. XIII, no. 1 (1959), pp. 38–59; B. G. Bechhoefer and E. Stein, "Atoms for Peace, the New IAEA," *Michigan Law Review*, Vol. 55, no. 6 (1957), pp. 747–798.

15. *Report of the Preparatory Commission of the International Atomic Energy Agency*, IAEA/GC.1/1.GOV/1, New York, 1957, p. 22.

16. IAEA/GC (IX) 294, April 21, 1965, par. 25.

17. See Article XII of the Agency Statute.

18. Article XII of the IAEA Statute which grants substantial authority to IAEA beyond that assumed in the three remaining documents; the Safeguards Document, GC(IX) 294 of April 21, 1965, which was approved by the IAEA General Conference in Tokyo in October 1965; the Inspectors' Document, GC(V)INF/39 of August 28, 1961, which is a series of instructions to inspectors administering both safeguards and health and safety; the Agreement on Privileges and Immunities of the Agency, INFCIRC/9/Rev. 1 of December 21, 1959.

19. This is the present practice of the U.S. Atomic Energy Commission.

CASE 2

1. In this study the terms nuclear "charges" and nuclear "warheads" are used synonymously. Since, in principle, only the explosive material itself, the "charge", distinguishes a nuclear warhead from a non-nuclear warhead, an agreement concerning control of nuclear weapons necessarily focuses on the nuclear charge. Moreover, from the viewpoint of verification the difference in size between a warhead and its charge (which requires some container in order to be capable of transportation and storage) is too slight to raise any practical problems.

2. In most instances it would be extremely difficult, if not impossible, to detect undeclared tactical missiles carrying nuclear warheads. With respect to U.S. weapons, the variety is such that some of them (LANCE: 3–30 mile range) are air and helicopter transportable; others (SERGEANT: 25–

75 mile range and PERSHING: 100–400 mile range) require special purpose vehicles (transporters, erectors, launchers, generators, check-out vans,
etc.). The former would require the closest possible inspection for detection
whereas the latter might be identified by the characteristic supporting
vehicles.

Soviet tactical weapons are also highly mobile, and detection would
probably require identification of particular special purpose vehicles such
as propellant trailers, erectors, launchers, etc. The problem might be considered as comparable to the detection of individual tanks for artillery
pieces.

3. Little progress has been made in developing a device for detecting
hidden stores of fissionable material since Oppenheimer's classic reply to
the Congress in 1946 that "a screwdriver, to open suspect crates, is the only
sure thing." This situation is partly owing to the small quantity and low
energy of radiation emitted by the three common fissionable materials; the
other factor is that much of the natural radioactive background of the
earth and the atmosphere is from uranium and its decomposition products
and it is thus very difficult to detect the presence of a little more uranium
against this background. There seems to be little basis for assuming this
situation will improve.

4. For the purpose of identification, the verification organization made
up of the Western states (and possibly including international personnel)
will be referred to as the Western Verification Organization. The verification
organization made up of the Soviet Union and other appropriate interested East European socialist countries (and possibly international personnel) will be referred to as the Eastern Verification Organization. It
should be noted, however, that as long as France's place in NATO remains
uncertain, the feasibility of this organizational scheme for inspection must
be scrutinized with special care.

5. Mindful of the Soviet sensitivity to symmetry, the asymmetrical figure
of 1063 personnel favoring the Western Verification Organization can be
justified as follows. The area to be inspected by the Western Verification
Organization in Czechoslovakia, East Germany, and Poland totals approximately 211,360 square miles. The area to be inspected by the Eastern Verification Organization in West Germany totals approximately 95,930
square miles. On the basis of personnel strengths of the respective organizations (497 and 1063) the ratio of personnel to the respective area of responsibility for the Western Verification Organization is one person per
198 square miles and for the Eastern Verification Organization one person
per 193 square miles.

CASE 3

1. United States Arms Control and Disarmament Agency, Publication 23,
Agenda Item—Peace (Washington: Government Printing Office, July 1964),
p. 2. See also: The Bendix Corporation, *Verification Requirements for
Restorations on Strategic Nuclear Delivery Vehicles* (ACDA/ST–6, July
1964). Jeremy J. Stone, *Containing the Arms Race: Some Specific Proposals*
(Cambridge, Mass: MIT Press, 1966), pp. 179–216.

2. The facilities to be declared would include the following:

a) Facilities performing final production-line assembly of the armaments or vehicles in the affected categories. However, this would not be

interpreted to include military installations not engaged in manufacturing at which partial assembly or disassembly might be performed for operational or maintenance purposes.

b) Facilities producing the specified major sub-assemblies—that is, those producing or testing ballistic-missile liquid-fueled engines or solid-fueled motors; those fabricating and assembling tankage, and ballistic-missile stage assemblies and mobile launchers; and those manufacturing aircraft or cruise-type missile fuselages.

c) Facilities manufacturing ship hulls used for launching sea-based missiles. See ENDC/PV. 211, August 27, 1964, pp. 6–7.

3. See, for example, the data accumulation proposed in a study prepared by the Institute for International Order, *Factory Inspection and Armaments Control* (New York, 1956).

4. The Bendix Corporation, *Techniques for Monitoring Production of Strategic Delivery Vehicles*, Vol. I, *Technical Inspection Procedures*, ACDA–1 (Ann Arbor, Michigan: January 1960), pp. 1–5.

5. ENDC/PV.211, pp. 5–6.

6. *Ibid.*, p. 6.

7. Verification as to whether modifications were being tested could be provided by other sources.

8. Launching facilities associated with strategic anti-missile-missile systems will not be treated in this study because it is the U.S. position that further technical discussions will be required in order to formulate a workable and acceptable definition of "anti-missile-missile systems."

9. We use the term "reciprocal" rather than "adversary." The meaning of the terms is identical for the purposes of this study.

10. Each Regional Office should be so located that the resident teams under its jurisdiction are within a one-day travel distance by road. Consideration should also be given to making the regions congruous with existing military or political regions of the host country, if such a deployment were advantageous to the operation of the inspecting organization.

CASE 4

1. ENDC/PV.35, May 11, 1962.

2. Presumably, the "specified" parties would include all states having significant quantities of the kinds of armaments to be reduced.

3. ENDC/PV.35, May 11, 1962.

4. See letter of September 20, 1961, from Deputy Foreign Minister Zorin to Presidential Adviser McCloy, in *Documents on Disarmament, 1961*, p. 443.

5. ENDC/PV.114, March 27, 1963.

6. This is a gesture toward a modest reduction of the weapons stockpiles of the two powers. The amounts have not been specified, but transfers in the amount of 60,000 kilograms of weapons grade U–235 by the United States and 40,000 kilograms by the Soviet Union have been mentioned.

7. ENDC/PV.36, May 14, 1962.

8. ENDC/53, August 1, 1962.

9. ENDC/53, August 1, 1962.

10. ENDC/PV.48, June 4, 1962.

11. Ciro E. Zoppo, *The Accession of Other Nations to the Nuclear Test Ban Treaty* (Santa Monica, Calif.: The RAND Corp., 1963), p. 24.

12. Representation in the ENDC is as follows: (1) The Soviet Union and four of its allies; (2) five members of NATO (although France has

refused to participate); (3) eight other members—two from Latin America, two from Asia, two from sub-Saharan Africa, one Arab state, and one from "Western" Europe.

13. One device that has been relatively successful in satisfying states that their interests would be protected even though they were not represented on the executive organ has been to accord members the right to participate in the discussion on any matters of special interest to them. Such a right should be included in the IDO Statute.

14. ENDC/PV.21, April 16, 1962.

15. U.S. Department of State, *Geneva Conference on the Discontinuance of Nuclear Weapons Tests: History and Analysis of Negotiations,* (October, 1961), pp. 198–199. Hereinafter cited as *Geneva Conference: History and Analysis.*

16. See in particular the Anglo-American Draft Treaty of April 18, 1961, in *Documents on Disarmament, 1961,* p. 82ff.

17. See *Geneva Conference: History and Analysis,* p. 443ff.

18. The matter might also be brought as a dispute or situation likely to endanger the maintenance of international peace and security under Chapter VI.

PART II

DESIGNS FOR AN INTERNATIONAL ARMS CONTROL ORGANIZATION

Chapter 1

1. The Antarctic region has already been denuclearized. No international organizational arrangements were considered necessary in this case, probably in view of the simple requirements for verification. The recently negotiated Latin American Nuclear Free Zone Treaty is another example of regional denuclearization.

2. M.I.T., Center of International Studies, *Regional Arms Control Arrangements for Developing Areas* (Cambridge, Mass.: 1964), Chap. VII, p. 3.

3. Article XII of the Amended Agreement for Cooperation, effective July 9, 1962. 13 *United States Treaties and other International Agreements* 1439.

4. See Articles III.A.5, VIII.B, and XII.A.6 of the IAEA Statute.

5. This will be the case of the organization established to administer the Latin American Nuclear Free Zone Treaty, if that instrument enters into force.

Chapter 2

1. The composition of the staff might be determined in part by the nature of the inspection system. If, for example, the organization is to supply international observers to serve with reciprocal inspection teams, those observers would have to be drawn from nationals of states that are not aligned with either of the sides involved.

2. C. Wilfred Jenks, *International Immunities* (New York: Oceana Publications, 1961), pp. 131, 156–57.

3. Harold K. Jacobson and Eric Stein, *Diplomats, Scientists and Politicans: The United States and the Nuclear Test Ban Negotiations* (Ann Arbor: University of Michigan Press, 1966), p. 310ff.

4. *Executive authority* refers to the authority granted to the head of an

inspection organization for the direction, coordination, and control of the various elements of the organization. The organization head may be identified by many titles; e.g., Secretary-General, Administrative Executive, Administrator, Director-General, Inspector General. *Control* as used here refers to the authority which may be less than full executive authority exercised by the head of an organization over a portion of the activities of subordinate or other organizations. Consideration here is limited to administrative and operational control.

5. *Coordinating authority* is that authority which is vested in an individual to require consultation on the part of one or more organizations (or elements thereof) for coordinating specific functions or activities such as designating objectives, methods, and procedures to be followed in an inspection task. In the event the individual vested with this authority is unable to obtain essential agreement, he should refer the matter to his sponsor. In the absence of prior agreement, this authority would not include such matters as administration, discipline, internal organization, and training unless the elements over which this authority is exercised request assistance.

6. *Operational control* includes direction or exercise of authority involving the composition of subordinate units, assignment of tasks, designation of objectives, and the authoritative direction necessary to accomplish the mission. In the absence of prior agreement, it does not include functions such as administration, discipline, internal organization, and unit training unless the element over which this authority is exercised requests assistance.

7. *Administrative control* includes the direction or exercise of authority over subordinate or other organizations with respect to administrative matters such as personnel management, supply, services, and other matters not included in the operational missions of the subordinate or other organizations.

8. The agreements between the U.S. Atomic Energy Commission and the first commercial processing plant include such a formula to defray the cost of the accountability system. For special reasons, not relevant to this discussion, it was necessary to provide that the U.S. Government defray any additional expense arising from international safeguards.

9. Another factor is that the parties to an arms control or disarmament agreement are unlikely to be identical with the membership of the United Nations.

Chapter 4

1. Methods of responding to violations of arms control agreements are explored in great detail in a study completed in April 1968 for the U.S. Arms Control and Disarmament Agency. The study was directed by David W. Wainhouse, in association with B. G. Bechhoefer, W. E. Butler, A. P. Simons, and Arnold Wolfers. See *Alternative Methods for Dealing with Breaches of Arms Control Agreements*, 5 Vols., ACDA Cont. IR–107, April 1968.

Chapter 5

1. Neither the United States Senate nor the U.S.S.R. Council of Ministers is likely to accept an arrangement without retaining a veto over matters of vital concern to each.

INDEX

THE JOHNS HOPKINS PRESS

Designed by Gerard A. Valerio

Composed in Times Roman by Monotype Composition Company

Printed offset by Universal Lithographers, Inc. on P & S, R

Bound by L. H. Jenkins, Inc. in Columbia Fictionette, FNV–3927

DATE DUE
